M000222818

PRAISE FOR

GENERAL IN COMMAND

"A resplendent navy wool tunic and a silver scabbard. A West Point cadet's 'boat cloak;' pristine riding boots; photos of 'Ike' and Winston Churchill. All help tell the story of a heroic American. He not only witnessed history, he helped create it."

—CHARITA GOSHAY, Repository Editor, Canton, Ohio

"In *General In Command,* Van Ness presents a vivid biography of Major General John B. Anderson and his rise to the top. From Iowa farm to West Point, from chasing Pancho Villa to the trenches of France, from Fort Benning to XVI Corps Command, if you would like to understand how Anderson and the U.S. Army evolved, grew, and prevailed in World War II, this book is an excellent place to start."

—AMBASSADOR FRANK LAVIN, author of *Home Front to Battlefront: An Ohio Teenager in World War II*

"Frankly, I'm a bit jealous. My grandfather was General Malin Craig, Army Chief of Staff, 1935-1939. Van Ness did for his grandfather what my siblings and I were never able to do for ours: produce a great biography. More power to you, Mike."

—MR. PETER CRAIG, Bethesda, Maryland, Landon School for Boys, Class of 1972

"Van Ness weaves a fine story of an immigrant farm boy from Iowa who became both a family man and a warrior. From Van Ness' days as a young lad gazing at a photo in his grandfather's back hall, he sought to answer this boyhood question: 'Why was Granddaddy with Winston Churchill in a landing craft crossing the Rhine?' Here's the answer."

—MR. BROOKE ANDERSON, Curator Staff, MAPS Air Museum, North Canton, Ohio

"A great read!"

—MICHAEL P. HOPKINS, MD, West Point Class of 1971

"By the end of the book, I had tears in my eyes and a lump in my throat . . . I marvel at the flair of your writing."

—MRS. YVONNE WILLAMAN, Army Wife

General in Command:
The Life of Major General
John B. Anderson
by Michael M. Van Ness

© Copyright 2019 Michael M. Van Ness

ISBN 978-1-63393-849-6

All rights reserved. No part of this publication may be reproduced, stored in a retrieval system, or transmitted in any form or by any means—electronic, mechanical, photocopy, recording, or any other—except for brief quotations in printed reviews, without the prior written permission of the author.

Published by

 köehlerbooks™

210 60th Street
Virginia Beach, VA 23451
800–435–4811
www.koehlerbooks.com

GENERAL IN COMMAND

FROM IOWA FARM TO COMMAND OF THE
LARGEST COMBAT CORPS IN WORLD WAR II

THE LIFE OF MAJOR GENERAL
JOHN B. ANDERSON

MICHAEL M. VAN NESS

VIRGINIA BEACH
CAPE CHARLES

TABLE OF CONTENTS

to the memory of
Sue Palmer Anderson,
and all military wives

PREFACE

*"We are ever prouder of our ancestors than they would be of us,
were they to come back here and look in on us."*

—From a 1937 Letter from Nels Anderson
to His Younger Brother

I wrote this book to honor Major General John B. Anderson. When I started the project, I knew something of his military achievements but little of the man. As the project progressed, I discovered the trials and tribulations of a West Point graduate who rose through the ranks to rub elbows with the giants of the United States Army in the first half of the twentieth century. More importantly, I uncovered the story of a man and his family, a husband and father, and an officer and a gentleman. Along with his many achievements, he suffered bitter disappointments and grew disillusioned. He descended into the depths of alcoholism, withdrew from the world, and came nearly alone to his final resting place in Arlington National Cemetery.

While writing this book, I learned that he was a much more complicated man than the grandfather I knew as a youth. Despite his modest farm-boy upbringing, he was an outstanding student at West Point and an honor graduate of the Army Command and General Staff College at Fort Leavenworth. He was orphaned as a young officer and was divorced on his way to France in the First World War. I learned that he attended and advised the most senior United States diplomats about the details of the Geneva Convention of 1929 and that during the lonely years of Army service in the 1930s, he endured fourteen long years with no promotion. True to his commitment to academic excellence, he excelled as a teacher at the Army Command and General Staff College at Fort Leavenworth where he taught many of the combat leaders with whom he served in the field in Europe in World War II. I learned that he organized both the 102nd Infantry Division and the XVI Corps into effective fighting units. On his way to war, he dined with Prime Minister Winston Churchill, who he later escorted over the Rhine River. Finally, I learned that General Anderson commanded the largest United States Army Corps in combat in World War II in decisive victories against the Germans.

Nanny and Granddaddy visiting our family in Point Mugu 1957

He witnessed the horrors of modern warfare with the killing, wounding, and maiming of friends and foes, combatants and noncombatants, adults and children. He saw the reality of total war where the lines between civilians and soldiers were blurred. He was forced to reconcile the pain and anger he felt toward the Germans with the ideals he espoused during the Geneva Convention of 1929.

As the American Army advanced into the Netherlands, he encountered evidence of systematic mass starvation of the Dutch by the German Army. As the American Army advanced into Germany, he toured concentration camps, displaced persons' camps, and forced labor camps. He saw firsthand the consequences of industrialized mass killing at the camps situated among the well-fed German populace.

Even as these horrors were revealed, he was forced to turn a blind eye to the actions of rearguard units of the American Army that were committing their own atrocities. In the winter and spring of 1945, the Allies were responsible for the Rhineland prisoner of war camps, which held thousands of German prisoners of war. The Rhineland camps were no better than the worst POW camps in Germany containing Allied prisoners of war. Fields of mud, inadequate shelter and water supplies, little food, and widespread death from disease, neglect, starvation, and deliberate killings were common. The Allies could be as ruthless as their foes. General Anderson's knowledge of the American Army's role in these atrocities was never discussed, but his knowledge of these acts shook his faith in the institutions to which he committed his life.

His faith in his fellow officers, especially his most senior commanders, was also shaken. Compared to the horrors of the prisoner of war camps, the slight of being overlooked or neglected for promotion to a rank commensurate with his service may seem small, but it added insult to injury. Stoically, he endured the oversight of the Supreme Allied Commander, General Dwight Eisenhower. The reason for this oversight is unknown. Was it an old slight from West Point days when General Anderson was a year senior to the younger General Eisenhower, jealousy that General Anderson served overseas during World War I while General Eisenhower stayed stateside, or simple neglect during a confusing time at the end of the war when everyone just wanted to go home? We can only speculate.

As Supreme Allied Commander, Eisenhower wielded immense power over the careers of the officers under his command. Later, he held the highest position in the Army, Army Chief of Staff, a position that controlled the fortunes of all officers in the Army. In both circumstances, Eisenhower failed to promote Anderson to the rank commensurate with his service.

General Anderson never complained openly of this oversight. He was one to let his actions speak for themselves. He did not engage in self-promotion or seek publicity in the news media. In later years, in private letters, he wondered what steps might be taken to correct the record. Other officers were receiving the promotions commensurate with their service. Congressional action corrected Eisenhower's failure to recommend promotion of several four-star general officers, notably General William H. Simpson, Anderson's immediate superior in the field in Europe. Even with the election of Eisenhower to President of the United States, nothing was done. I know this oversight rankled for years and years.

Anderson's modest Iowa upbringing and his commitment to the West Point ideals of duty, honor, and country prepared him inadequately for the politics of the time. He was at sea among those officers who exploited their positions of trust with indulgences of luxurious camps and caravans, Riviera retreats, and grandiose entourages like those of Supreme Headquarters Allied Expeditionary Force personnel.

The principles of West Point and Outward Bound guided him. Duty, honor, and country were the priorities of his military service. Both in times of triumph and in the lonely times, the motto of Outward Bound, "To serve, to strive, and not to yield," guided his actions.

Other more personal advice served him well. His older brother Nels wrote in 1937 to then-Lieutenant Colonel Anderson these words: "We are ever prouder of our ancestors than they would be of us, were they to come back here and look in on us." Nels was more than twenty years older than his youngest sibling and something of a father figure. When this letter was written, Lieutenant Colonel Anderson was in his late forties, teaching at the Army Command and General Staff College, and wondering about his future service. The wartime army was small and paid regularly but poorly, the prospects of promotion were low, and there were few troops to command. Anderson was stuck in a dead-end job, wondering about the value of his life's work in the Army. Like many of us at that stage in life, the prospects at home and at work seemed to be diminishing. He sought counsel from his older brother.

I look at those words—"We are ever prouder of our ancestors than they would be of us, were they to come back here and look in on us"— and contemplate the meaning they had for my grandfather. Although he may have wondered whether his life was worthy of admiration by his own ancestors, I believe his brother was encouraging him to look to the future, not to dwell on the past. I believe his brother sensed greatness in his little brother that future generations would come to appreciate and admire. His brother was encouraging his youngest sibling to continue to strive for greatness, to serve proudly, and to yield to no one.

Those words carried a warning to my grandfather and carry a warning to us. The warning is this: Do not look to your ancestors for admiration. Do not think that your ancestors will understand you or your actions. Do not hold yourself hostage to your notion of what your ancestors would think of you. I believe Nels Anderson was telling his younger brother, and us, to seek our own counsel, to follow the tenets of our own lives, and to be confident in our own judgment. The words, the message, and the encouragement are prophetic and powerful.

In the end, as the years slipped by, General Anderson found comfort and solace in both alcohol and prayer. At the time I knew him, I understood little of his need to drink and to pray. As I learned during the writing of this book, the rewards of faith and prayer and the value of the long journey of the soldier of the Great War are real. My grandfather struggled honestly to find meaning in the great war of life. His struggle transcends all the honors other men could bestow. I am honored to write this book of the service of Major General John B. Anderson, my grandfather. I hope the reader will likewise be rewarded.

CHAPTER I

IOWA CHILDHOOD

1891-1910

John Benjamin Anderson was born March 10, 1891, in Parkersburg, Iowa, the youngest son of Carl Christian and Louise Christine Frederica Simonsen.[1]

His siblings were: half-brother, Frederik; sisters Hanna, Symona, Amelia, and Margaret; and older brother Nels,[2] who, among his brother and sisters, plays the most prominent role in this history of his life.

John B. Anderson, age 3, 1894

Nels Anderson was a member of the Iowa National Guard, participated in the Spanish-American War, and contracted yellow fever in Cuba. In later life, he lived in San Francisco, where he experienced the great earthquake and fire in 1906. He lost most of his personal possessions in those disasters. At sixty-seven years old, he died in May 1942, in San Francisco, of congestive heart failure attributed to the yellow fever he contracted during the Spanish-American War. He would be a great source of inspiration to his younger brother.

Nels Anderson circa 1899

Although John Benjamin Anderson's first name is John, as evidenced here and elsewhere, his family and friends in Parkersburg often called him "Ben." He was the youngest son of an immigrant laborer and farmer. His early life was typical of farm boys of his generation . . . hard labor on the farm, school, chores, church, and family. The risks of childhood diseases were ever-present. He escaped the worst of them like diphtheria, tuberculosis, and polio, but his niece Louisa Richardson was not so lucky and lived with the consequences of polio for the rest of her life. Young "Ben" grew to five-foot-eight with the lean, muscular build of an Iowan wrestler. Beyond two childhood photos, the first documented event in his young life was a newspaper article from March 1910, detailing his departure to West Point. It read:

> "Benj. Anderson left Monday night for Chicago to visit a sister for a few days. From that place, he goes direct to West Point to enter the U.S. Military Academy as a cadet. He will not get home again until two years from next June. Ben's many friends in Parkersburg believe that he will have no trouble in making good at that institution. The work is hard, but Ben is an exceptionally bright young man and a good student and these qualifications count for much with the military authorities in charge of the school."

His family must have been bursting with pride at his having attained this opportunity. Fewer than 130 cadet candidates received appointments to West Point in 1910. Appointment to the service academies is the prerogative of United States senators, representatives, and state governors. Each official has the privilege of an annual appointment. Whether an interested teacher or minister assisted young Ben in his selection is unknown. His brother Nels' service in the Iowa National Guard in the Spanish-American War may have been a source of inspiration but was unlikely to have opened any doors for his little brother.

Many Midwestern boys sought out a life in the military. Some boys had fathers and grandfathers with a history of distinguished service. For example, Douglas MacArthur, United States Military Academy (USMA) 1903, born in Little Rock, Arkansas, was the son of a decorated Civil War hero who received the Congressional Medal of Honor for exploits on Missionary Ridge in November 1863. Other boys like John J. Pershing, USMA 1886, Dwight D. Eisenhower, USMA 1915, and Omar N. Bradley, USMA 1915, were likely seeking a better life for themselves.

However it came about, "Ben" Anderson was on his way. He would see his mother alive just one more time, in the summer of 1912, during his summer furlough between his second and third years at West Point. He would see his father alive but three more times, in 1912, in 1914 after his West Point graduation, and in 1915 during service with General John J. Pershing on the Texas-Mexico border. After his father's death in 1917, he was an orphan, the youngest boy in a family scattered across the United States, and in many ways alone in the world.

CHAPTER 2

WEST POINT

1910-1914

The Army became Ben Anderson's family. The summer-long initiation rite of Beast Barracks or "Beastdom" and the yearlong ordeal of the plebe year or "Plebedom" awaited Cadet Anderson. Despite his Danish heritage, he acquired a new nickname: "Swede." He was determined to achieve success.

In 1910, life at West Point was monastic. No cadet could marry. No cadet could live off campus. No cadet could accept a monetary gift. The honor code governed daily life. Every day was scheduled from reveille to lights out. Deadlines were numerous and were expected to be met. Room inspections were both scheduled and random. Military rituals and formations, chapel services, initiation rites, and institutional history were taken seriously and followed with devotion. The powerful institutional indoctrination is not easily understood by the outsider.

The West Point yearbook, *The Howitzer*, details the lives of the cadets. Athletic and martial skills, mathematical prowess, and engineering expertise were celebrated in the 1914 edition. A cartoon from *The Howitzer* shows Cadet Anderson receiving some unwanted attention on the rifle range. A sense of humor and an appreciation

Anderson, J. B., (at gallery practice). He makes a possible and on the next clip gets a bunch of low fours.

Tac: "What's the matter, Mr. Anderson?"

B. J.: "I guess the target was moved up higher, sir. It was all right before."

Cartoon of Cadet Anderson on the Rifle Range

of "the absurd" helped him and the other young men cope with the stress of daily life, with its constant grading, formality, and scrutiny.

While athletic participation and martial skills were most important, literary societies, dances, and extracurricular activities were needed to round out the cadets' training and experience to make them "officers and gentlemen."

In 1911, his brother Nels, a self-published poet, sent him a copy of his poetry. The verses were fitting for a West Point cadet at the beginning of his training and career and dwell on the loneliness of separation, the horrors of war, and the power of prayer.

To Ben
from his brother
Jno. D. Anderson

11/10/11

Inscription in the Voice of the Infinite

"Epitaph to a Soldier" from *The Voice of the Infinite*

And now the rain beats down upon his grave;
The wild beasts snarl and sniff above the mound;
Aloft the vulture circles round and round;
Deep in the bushes lurks the human knave.

Cadet Anderson Mourning, 1913

'Twas such a place as this, and such a land,
We laid him whom the Morn proclaimed her pride,
A soldier battle-scarred and brave and grand,
Who ere the day had wheeled sank low and died.

Rest to his soul! He wrought the best he could,
And doing thus had made him truly good.
Peace to his bones! He was a peaceful man,
Though every battle found him in the van;
In midst of evil, yet from evil free—
Let him who reads pray thus he, too may be.

THE ARMY MULE.

Cadet Anderson (left) with Army Mule Army-Navy Game, 1913

Cadet Anderson's mother, Louise, died on June 22, 1913. She had endured the hardships of frontier life, arriving in Iowa on the Great Plains in 1882 but ten years after the end of the Indian Wars. She had borne six children and seen them properly raised, educated, and married. She saw her youngest son return to West Point in the summer of 1912 knowing she might never see him again.

During the Army-Navy Game in November 1913, First Class Cadet Anderson attended the Army mule throughout the game. His 1914 *Howitzer* entry confirms that he was the "Curator of the Army Mule" in the 1913 football season—probably because of his farm upbringing.

His *Howitzer* page also says, "He hates plebes worse than Charlie the Barber[3] does the Cubs." This suggests that the Class of 1915 plebes, including Dwight Eisenhower and Omar Bradley, found "Swede" Anderson a firm taskmaster during Beast Barracks. He was singled out for "his efficient handling of the First-Class Cavalry Hike." He held positions of responsibility in the corps hierarchy, first as corporal, then

**Cadet Anderson (sixth from the right in the second rank)
with West Point Class of 1914**

as acting sergeant. These were not officer positions but nevertheless demonstrate leadership potential. His roommate, or "wife" in West Point parlance, was Charles M. Milliken. The statement "He was never been presented with an A.B." (Area Bird) was made about Swede. An "Area Bird" is one who has received demerits for violations of military conduct. This person has to "work off" the demerits by walking in circles around the parade ground, often for hours regardless of weather.

So, he kept his nose clean. His motto—"Take a chance"—suggests

Cadet Anderson Yearbook Page

that given the right circumstances, he would follow his own counsel. *The Howitzer* depicts a careful man, fond of animals, hard on plebes, and accepting of responsibility. This description seems to fit.

Cadet Anderson's final report card placed him at number thirty-two out of 107 in his class—the top third. Class rank determined the branch of the Army the cadet could choose. He chose field artillery.

Each year, West Point graduation occurs during June

Week, a bucolic time along the upper Hudson River. The members of the Class of 1914 heard United States Secretary of War Lindley M. Garrison of New Jersey say:

> *"The Army officer starts off with an education and a spirit. He learns to control others by learning self-control. He learns that no orderly government is possible unless the citizen exercises self-control and submits to proper discipline. He learns to do whatever he is set to do, and to do it with all that is in him. He learns to take orders and to carry them out, and to give orders and insist upon obedience. And, finally, he learns that in no rank of life and in no field of endeavor can any man do better or go further than in his own, where his motto always has been and always will be 'Honor, valor, and vigor.'"*

Among the guests at graduation was John J. Pershing, USMA Class of 1886. He was there to honor his sister Grace's son Richard Paddock's graduation. Pershing was the hero of the day. In 1914, he had returned from the Philippines having successfully suppressed the Moro Rebellion and negotiated a peace treaty among the warring factions. More recently, he had been assigned the duty by President Woodrow Wilson of security of the Texas-Mexico border, the border being threatened by warring factions in Mexico's ongoing civil war. Knowing he was going to need young officers to serve along the border, Pershing likely took great interest in the graduates of the Class of 1914.

Immediately upon graduation, a West Point cadet receives his commission as a second lieutenant in the Army. The ceremony is usually performed by an active duty officer, a favored faculty member, or a West Point alumnus. Typically, the commissioning ceremony takes place among the monuments and statues of famous generals overlooking the Hudson River. It can be a solemn occasion marked by tears of joy and sorrow. In Cadet Anderson's case, graduation must have been a bittersweet time. He had excelled and grown in strength and confidence. He had a future as an officer and a gentleman. He had survived a difficult, competitive, and lonely indoctrination into the oldest branch of the United States military. Unfortunately, no family member from Iowa would make the trip to New York to see him graduate from West Point.

Second Lieutenant John B. Anderson's military service was to affect many of his family over the next generations. It was one chapter of a larger book of family military service. As mentioned previously, his brother Nels served in the Spanish-American War. Later, John B. Anderson's only daughter would marry a graduate of the US Naval Academy. Two of his grandsons would serve in the military, one in the Army and one in the Navy.

Anderson may have joined out of a sense of duty or as a means of seeking adventure. He may have sought financial stability beyond the life of a farmer and sought a sense of greater purpose. Regardless of his motivation, at the time he swore the Oath of Allegiance to the United States, his service was a quiet example of the meaning behind the previously mentioned words of the Secretary of War, or even more succinctly, by the motto of West Point: "Duty, Honor, Country."

CHAPTER 3

THE MEXICAN INCURSION

1914-1917

A fter graduation from West Point on June 12, 1914, Second Lieutenant Anderson returned home to Iowa for a two-month leave. This visit was the first one since the death of his mother in June 1913 and must have been a sad reunion with his father, his siblings, and their children. After his leave was over, he departed Iowa for duty on the southwest border of Texas and joined his unit, the United States Sixth Field Artillery Regiment.

REGIMENTAL COAT OF ARMS

Regimental Cout of Arms, Sixth Field Artillery, 1914

To wearers of the Sixth Field Artillery badge, the regimental crest evokes the Mexican War of 1846 and the American Civil War service of their predecessors. It serves as a reminder of their sacrifices and as an inspiration to continue its legacy. These regimental coats of arms were updated and modified as circumstances dictated. In 1914, the regimental coat of arms of the Sixth Field Artillery showed that the six batteries, A through F, were horse drawn. *"Celer et Audax"* means "Swift and Bold," meant to inspire the men to greatness.

As part of the forces for the protection of the Texas-Mexico border, the reorganized Sixth Field Artillery was placed under the command of General John J. Pershing. Upon reporting for duty with the Sixth Field Artillery in August 1914, Second Lieutenant Anderson and his West Point classmate Bill Houghton found themselves invited aboard General Pershing's car. It was for a ride with him to their first duty station, a nearby camp called "Camp Dust." It was the first time the two young officers had ever ridden in a car. As they arrived at Camp Dust in the general's car, a salute was fired in honor of General Pershing's arrival. Houghton and Anderson always claimed, tongue-in-cheek, that the salute was for the two new second lieutenants. In a tape recording fifty years later, retired Major General Anderson recalled the awful living conditions and an incident of sitting down by mistake on a cactus and "getting up in a hurry!" It was a miserable duty station; in the tape, he says he "never thought [he] would get out of the Southwest."

The border was hot, dusty, and hostile. Military force was deemed necessary to keep Mexican insurgents from entering the United States. While a political settlement with Mexico was the goal of the Woodrow Wilson administration, the Army on the border trained hard in the art and science of war. Maneuvers, live-fire demonstrations, and painstaking instruction of companies, battalions, and regiments prepared the officers and men for combat. Once, while observing the Mexicans off in the distance, an artillery shell from a Mexican cannon landed close by knocking Second Lieutenant Anderson and his friend John Starkey from their caisson. Neither was seriously wounded. The incident served to remind the young officers that Army service could be serious business.

• • •

Mexican political history relevant to the unrest of 1914 dates back to 1821, the date of the end of the First Mexican War of Independence. Once the largest and wealthiest colony of Spain, stretching from the Pacific to the Caribbean Sea, north to Oregon, and south to Central America, in 1921 Mexico declared itself independent and free. From its beginning, tensions existed between wealthy land owners who favored a strong central government and "republicans" who favored decentralized authority.

Revolution erupted in Mexico in 1910. Banditos swept Porfirio Diaz from the presidency, and for four years near anarchy gripped Mexico. *"Pistoleros"* vied for control of the country. The president of Mexico, the visionary patriot Francisco Madero, was assassinated by Victoriano Huerta who was determined to establish a strong central government under his own control. Huerta vowed to protect British oil interests, and Britain recognized him as the legitimate president of Mexico.

In 1913, newly elected Woodrow Wilson condemned the assassin Huerta as "evil incarnate, a creature beyond humanity." Venustiano Carrazana sought revenge for President Madero's murder. Pancho Villa and Alvaro Obregon joined Carrazana in opposition to Huerta. These two rebels operated in the arid north country. While Germany was supplying Huerta's forces with modern arms and ammunition, the forces of Carrazano and Villa wandered the northern desert with little logistical support beyond arms and supplies smuggled across the border.

The official policy of the United States was to remain neutral. In practice, the Mexican Federals commanded by Huerta and the Mexican rebels commanded by Carrazana smuggled arms over the US-Mexico border in ever-increasing quantities. In the confused diplomatic situation, President Wilson failed to provide the military on the US-Mexico border with clear orders.

**General John J. Pershing with General Obregon (left)
and Pancho Villa (center), 1914**

In the absence of clear guidance from Washington and in the face of increasing anxiety among the local populace along the border, General Pershing resorted to the art of personal diplomacy. Pershing knew that personal relations often yielded military allies. He had had success defusing conflict with American Indian foes and Philippine Moro rebels by sitting down and getting to know his adversaries.

Pershing strove for impartiality. Shortly after Second Lieutenant Anderson's arrival, Pershing met with followers of Victoriano Huerta. He also met with Carrazano supporters General Obregon and Pancho Villa.

Despite Wilson's personal inclination to support Pancho Villa as a true Mexican patriot, the president was forced to reconsider. Looking for food and arms, Pancho Villa began to raid towns across the United States border. Wilson needed to act to protect United States interests. He commanded Pershing and the Army to defend the border from Columbus, New Mexico, to Sierra Blanca, Texas. Pershing established his headquarters in El Paso on the border and gathered his forces.

Thus, Second Lieutenant Anderson now found himself stationed in El Paso. In the summer of 1914, El Paso was a frontier town, a crossroads of northern migrating Mexicans, American Indians, outlaw gunmen, and old Confederate veterans. El Paso had a long history of cross-border commerce, legal and illegal. Increasingly, it depended on the presence of the railroad and Fort Bliss. Like many towns dependent on the army, El Paso liked its warriors and opened its country club, civic associations, and homes to the officers and men of the Army, including the newly arrived Sixth Field Artillery.

El Paso held many charms for the newly arrived Sixth Field Artillery officer. The farm boy from Iowa, newly released from the monastic life of West Point, was introduced to Grace Amoleyetto Wingo. She was the eighteen-year-old daughter of a prominent banking family involved in the railroad business and all types of cross-border commerce. Anderson had the lean look of a soldier serving in a hot climate. After what can best be described as a whirlwind courtship, the young lieutenant and Grace Wingo were married on March 25, 1915, just west of El Paso, in another frontier town, Douglas, Arizona.

• • •

Lt. John B. Anderson with bride Grace Amoleyetto Wingo, wedding date, 25 March 1915

Beyond his personal life, now First Lieutenant Anderson's career began to unfold. Ever since war had erupted in Europe in August 1914, he must have wondered when the United States would get involved. Three years of active service and the opportunity to command in the field in Mexico opened doors for the young officer.

On April 6, 1917, the United States declared war on Germany. To aid our allies, President Wilson selected General Pershing to command the First Division and take it to France. The Sixth Field Artillery Regiment was incorporated into the First Division. Upon the regiment's deployment to France, the regimental coat of arms was altered by the addition of a crimson "1" on a field of olive drab to denote its incorporation into the First Division.

REGIMENTAL COAT OF ARMS

Sixth Field Artillery of the First Division, 1917

In 1917, now-Captain JohnAnderson was selected to join Pershing in the first wave of American troops headed for France in World War I. On July 31, 1917, he sailed with the Sixth Field Artillery and the First Division for France. He had married but was now divorced. The thought of his death in combat or the impending long months of separation had been too much for his young bride.

CHAPTER 4

WORLD WAR ONE

1917-1918

While abroad, Captain Anderson kept a diary. There is an evolution in the tone of his writings over the course of his ten months in the country. At the beginning, the diary reads chattily and breezily as though he was off on an adventure. And he was. During the Mexican incursion against an amateur army without modern weapons, the Sixth Field Artillery suffered few casualties and only random shots from their foe. Now that they were to engage a professional army with up-to-date weapons, the reality of modern warfare became increasingly clear to Captain Anderson.

Captain Anderson's World War I diary cover page, dated 1917, reads:

"Diary of John B. Anderson, Captain, 6th Field Artillery, U.S. Army

In case of my death, please send this diary to Mrs. Henry Johnson, Jr., P.O. Box #27, Parkersburg, Iowa."

Captain Anderson's WWI diary cover page, 1917

Mrs. Henry Johnson is the married name of Captain Anderson's sister Margaret who was married to Henry Janssen Johnson Jr. Since Anderson was now an orphan and divorced, his sister was the logical person to whom his personal effects would be sent in the event of his death.

For many young men going off to war, a "hearty" farewell and "jaunty" attitude toward their possible death are psychological mechanisms to control the fear and anxiety inherent in departure. The matter-of-fact nature of Captain Anderson's words masks in part the reality of the meaning of those words, especially in wartime. He had read for nearly three years of the meat-grinder of war on the Western Front. He knew this war was a different game.

The Sixth Field Artillery loaded aboard ship and departed in convoy from Hoboken, New Jersey. Captain Anderson must have realized that his departure from New York, just down the Hudson River from West Point, might possibly be his last view of the United States. The sight of the Statue of Liberty receding from sight as the convoy headed east to France must have tested his notion of manhood and courage.

MY DIARY

There are many things I would rather do than keep a diary, but I have at last started this one and I will do my best to make it as interesting as possible, yet, at the same time, telling things only as they happened.

There are two grand reasons why this diary cannot be successfully written and they are: First, I hate to write, and it has always been difficult for me to place my thoughts in writing, and, secondly, I am starting about six months late.

The first of these reasons cannot be remedied, but the second I will try to override to a small degree by giving a brief synopsis of the different events and occasions, which may be of interest to others, which have taken place since I left the U.S. So we're off!

Originally, we were supposed to sail June 15, 1917, but due to lack of transportation, or other reasons, we did not receive our actual orders to leave Douglas, Arizona, where my regiment was then stationed, until July 21st, or thereabouts. We were keen to go, and as our time was limited, we hustled around, and all of us were clear of Douglas inside of two days.

We had excellent train service all the way to Hoboken, reaching there in record time—about July 27th, I believe. We were immediately escorted to the transport—the Henry R. Mallory [4]—and at 2 o'clock the afternoon of the 27th we pulled away from the dock and sailed down the river about four miles, at which point we cast anchor to wait for the remainder of our convoy.

While lying in the river, one of our transports, the Saratoga, came to grief. It was a bright, clear day and there was no excuse for the accident. Really it looked as though a Boche might have been responsible, but we'll probably never know. At any rate, the Panama rammed her—the Saratoga, I mean—and punched a large hole in her. The Saratoga immediately began to sink, but with the aid of tugs, rowboats, motorboats, etc., all the soldiers on board were gotten off safely and quickly. She was then towed to the dry dock on the Brooklyn side.

Our regiment had a large quantity of baggage of various kinds on her, which we have not seen to this day.

On the morning of July 30th, at 2 a.m., we lifted our anchor, and our convoy, consisting of our own ship, the Tenedores and Pasadores, carrying the 5th and 7th F.A. respectively, a tanker, a cruiser, and three destroyers, started on our voyage to France.

The trip itself was quite pleasant and uneventful. The weather was perfect, except for a few foggy nights, when we were very much afraid we might ram another ship or our convoy or be rammed, but we got through them safely enough. Also, the second day out we had a submarine alarm, but it turned out to be a floating piece of timber instead of a periscope.

About two days off of France we were met by U.S. destroyers, whereupon our original protectors—the cruiser and three destroyers—turned about and started home.

We were now in the danger zone, but nothing happened, except that we doubled our vigilance and our lookouts.

Finally, on Aug. 12th, we saw land at about 8 a.m. in the morning, and all of us were exceedingly thankful that we had come through without misfortune. All day we dragged along at a snail's pace, very close to the shore, as St. Nazaire, our landing place is situated at the head of an inlet.

The scenery was beautiful, and it was hard to realize that this beautiful country was the scene of the most terrible, horrible and cruel wars of history.

The American Army in the summer of 1917 had few units capable of fighting a modern war. The officers and men would learn the realities of modern warfare by hard experience. General Pershing and his officers were determined to keep American soldiers under American command, not levies of soldiers demanded by the French and English generals for piecemeal incorporation into their armies. The officers and men of the American Army were truly "summertime" soldiers with a spring in their step and swelled chests who would soon learn the realities of trench warfare. The English armies were mired in the lowlands of Flanders and Belgium while the French were stretched thin across northern France to Switzerland. While the French countryside and cities were largely untouched directly by the war, the cost in terms of manpower and treasure were bankrupting the government. With the Russians in full collapse in the east and with the Russian Revolution in October 1917, the newly arrived Americans were soon to feel the weight of the German Army.

At about four o'clock we finally reached the canal which leads into the basin at St. Nazaire, and soon after we were being lifted in the lock to the level of the basin. Both sides of the lock were lined with French people who cheered wildly. So, our band, which had been playing all the way in, finally broke into "The Marseillaise"; whereupon the crowd yelled themselves hoarse. They called for Tipperary, too, which seemed strange to us, but the band played it for them, whereupon there was more yelling. Later I learned that the French are exceedingly fond of Tipperary.

Now that I was nearer France, I realized more and more that she was at war. Nearly every woman was in mourning; there were no young men in the throngs, nothing but cripples, women, children and old men.

It was here too that I first saw German prisoners. They were a healthy, fine-looking bunch of soldiers, and apparently only too glad to be so far away from the hell of the front.

We finally tied up at the dock at about 6 p.m., but as it was too late to disembark, we remained aboard that night, and disembarked early the next morning. The regiment was formed on the dock, and then marched to cantonments, with the band in the lead. In spite of the early hour the streets were lined with people who cheered us until they were hoarse.

We remained in St. Nazaire for about four or five days doing nothing but rest, with the exception of a few short drills. Also, we were trying to get what property we could find straightened out.

But finally, we were on our way again—this time to our training camp at Valdahon, an army post near the Swiss border, and about 20 miles from Besancon. It took us about 40 hours to make the trip, but every inch of it was interesting, for France is a beautiful country, and every city is more or less historic and interesting.

In the book called the *Sixth Regiment Field Artillery*, Captain John B. Anderson, then adjutant of the regiment, wrote in part:

> "Troop trains in France are standardized and consist of 50 cars, 30 box cars, or third-class coaches, 17 flats, 1 first-class coach for officers, and 2 cabooses for the train crew. The men travel in box cars—for one rarely sees third class coaches in troop trains—36-40 men in each car, and as the trucks are only about half the size of American cars, the crowding is unavoidable. Also, there are no means for cooking on the train and reserve rations must be placed in each car to feed the men en route. Hot coffee is served at certain stations, usually at from 6 to 8 intervals. Sleeping is quite impossible as the men are forced to stand up or sit upright on backless benches throughout the whole trip, so consequently, a long trip is very fatiguing for the men. This matter cannot be remedied, as we are entirely dependent on the French Government for rail transportation in France, and naturally that government is unwilling to alter the composition of military trains to meet our needs or requirements.
>
> "The regiment arrived at Valdahon at about ten o'clock at night, unloaded, and the men were marched to their barracks at the post."

At Valdahon we found a splendid arrangement of barracks for the men, barracks with large comfortable rooms for the officers, a real shower bath (the first I had seen since leaving the Mallory) and a good mess, and an excellent target range.

After two days in which to get settled, our new guns and horses began to arrive, whereupon we went to work. The guns were the famous French 75mm. guns for the 6th and 7th F.A., and 155mm. howitzers for the 5th F.A. The 75's are popularly known throughout France as the "soixante quinze", meaning 75. It is a very old model —1897 but so good that it has never been altered except in one minor detail—the range disc.

We started work with a will, and with the assistance of a group of French officers, called the French mission, soon learned the French (and trench) methods of obtaining firing data, mastered the few differences which the new gun offered over our own 3-inch, and fired hundreds of rounds daily.

The men enjoyed the work apparently, as did the officers, in spite of mud and rain, which is always in the ascendency in France.

In the meantime, our Colonel —W.S. McNair—was made a brigadier general and took me for his aide-de-camp. We took many trips in his automobile, and I saw a lot of that particular section of France. Besancon, for instance, is a very interesting old place. It was captured by Caesar in his time, and many of the old Roman ruins still remain. We went to see them, and they were well worth the trip. Also, we went to the Swiss border, and though we could not cross, yet I am sure I had at least one foot on Swiss territory. We went to the source of the Loire, which is a river which flows out of the side of a hill, through a very deep gorge—almost as wonderful as our own Grand Canyon. Also, we went to see the "Glacier", which is a deep cave—about 200 feet deep—in which ice forms the year round.

"Joe" Swing, class of 1915, and in the Field Artillery, was aide to Gen. March and we used to go off on motorcycle trips also to various places. It was on one of these trips that we hit an ox-cart and were both thrown onto a manure-pile. We were knocked completely out, and were brought home by a peasant. I came to twelve hours later and had no more idea than a rabbit as to what had happened. The motorcycle was unhurt. You can imagine the odor which persisted in staying with me for weeks.

At Valdahon I took my first aero plane flight—also several other flights. It is great and I have wished many times since that I were an aviator. But the Field Artillery game is a good one too, so why wish for something else.

About October 1st, I received my order making me a captain from May 15th. Lots of back pay, which was welcome. Also, this automatically relieved me as aide-de-camp, for a Brig. Gen. cannot have a Capt. as an aide. But Gen. McNair was also ordered back to the States at about the same time so I would have lost the job anyway.

Well, I returned to the regiment and was made Adjutant. The training continued—not only target practice, but aero plane and balloon observation, digging gun pits, construction of camouflage, wireless, etc.—until about October 20th when we received confidential orders stating we would go to the front for a certain period to complete our training which was good news to all of us.

But before I go on with our experiences at the front, I will interpolate a few impressions of France which I have received. To begin with, it is beautiful. The road system is wonderful all throughout France—the best I have ever seen. The country is intensely cultivated, except the wooded areas, of course, which are very numerous and extensive. There are very few isolated farms, as all the farmers gather in small villages, which cover the country. The villages at a distance—with their massive churches with tall spires, always present—are very picturesque, but at closer quarters they are filthy, smelly places, with cows, chickens, pigs and sheep filling the streets. Also, the manure heaps fill half the street, for among the peasant class, a man's wealth is judged from the size of the manure pile which adorns his portion of the street. (But I'll not complain about them, for, as you saw in a preceding page, one of them doubtless saved my worthless neck from being broken.) Also, the stable is always in the same building in which the human beings of the family live.

The railroad system of France is government-owned, and the service as a rule is slow, uncertain and very poor, perhaps due to war conditions. The locomotives look like toys, compared with our powerful types, and the freight cars are little things, about one-third the size of our smallest cars. The passenger coaches are divided into compartments, and you enter by a door in the side of the car—one door for each compartment.

On some of the Paris trains, the cars are slightly more modern, but none compare with ours at home. Then the coaches are divided into 1st, 2nd, and 3rd class coaches. The 1st and 2nd are alike, so far as I can see, except as to color of the upholstering; but the 3rd class have only plain board seats, without upholstery of any kind. During the war, all military people get a special rate, so that we can travel first class for less than one cent a mile.

The money system is difficult for an American who thinks in dollars. Everything is francs here—a franc is worth about 17 cents—and the franc is equal to 100 centimes. Of course, no centimes are made—only 5 centime, 10 centime and 50 centime pieces are made below the franc. One sees very little silver money—war conditions—but everything is paper. They even make paper franc and 50 centime notes, which are a horrible nuisance.

Instead of our usual measurements we now have to contend with the meter, a little more than a yard; the centimeter, about 1/5 inch; the liter, slightly less than a quart; the kilogramme, about 2 ½ pounds, and the kilometer, about 1100 yards. However, it is queer how soon one begins to think in all these terms instead of the old.

Now, for our first experience at the front. Only one battalion from each artillery and infantry regiment were to be at the front at the same time, which gave each infantry battalion about ten days, and each artillery battalion two weeks. Our first battalion left on Oct. 20th for Nancy, near which place we were to go into the line; that is, along the Rhine-Marne Canal in the Arracourt region. This battalion was composed of Batteries "A", "B" and "C", and Major J. R. Starkey commanded the battalion.[5]

The *Sixth Regiment Field Artillery* goes into some depth as to the details of the first American fire of the war. As Captain Anderson stated, Major Starkey was in command with Major Hollingsworth as his adjutant. They met the battalion in St. Nicholas du Port, near Jarville, a suburb of Nancy. Upon their arrival at the horse line, or echelon, the battalion went into billets and until well into the night, the town was in an uproar over the arrival of the first American troops.

According to the plan adopted, each American battery was under French command, in this case under the command of French Major Villars. Not a single shot could be fired without French permission. On the morning of the 22nd, fog obscured the German observation balloons, so every man with a pick and shovel prepared the gun pits. After an exhausting day of work, Major Starkey visited the men in their quarters. He hesitated to ask more of them that night. But if the Sixth Field Artillery was to be the first unit to fire into German lines, the guns would need to be installed in position that night. Other batteries had preceded the Sixth into position and undoubtedly were prepared to fire in the morning. He explained the urgent need for haste and asked for volunteers. With a whoop, he related that the entire detail responded.

The gun had to be picked up and carried. Although a relatively easy task for forty men, only a dozen were able to get a hold on the gun at a time. The wheels of the gun carriage sank to the axles, and ropes were needed to make them budge. The men were bogged down in the mud to their knees. Gas drifted in from a recent German bombardment requiring the donning of gas masks. Lieutenants joined in on the ropes, tugging like mules. Reaching the base of the hill, up which the gun was to be dragged, slippery clay slowed progress. But at last, with a final desperate heave, the gun was up and rolled into place. It was, said Major Starkey, the "hardest, nastiest, most back-breaking toil I had ever seen."

Dawn found a band of eager, anxious men assembled at the gun position. Beside the gun stood a picked crew, chosen among the men themselves. As the fog gradually lifted, Major Starkey gave them the necessary firing data of range and direction. With lanyard ready, the chief of the section verified the readings and at the command "Fire!" sent the shell winging its way into German territory.

There followed a continuous shifting in the makeup of the gun crew so that everyone present could have a hand in firing one or more shots. Twenty-four shells were sent over before the Americans ceased fire.

A report of the firing was sent by telephone to division headquarters. For a while the men knew not whether they had beaten their rival batteries. A few hours later, however, a messenger brought an order from General Sibert, their division commander, directing that the shell cases of the first eight shots fired that morning be sent to him. The first was immediately dispatched to President Wilson as a souvenir.

And what was our joy and pride when "C" Battery succeeded in firing the first shot into the Hun lines at 6:10 a.m., October 23rd, beating the 7th F.A. by only a very few minutes. The first cartridge case was carefully kept, and later sent to President Wilson as a memento of the first message sent over by the Americans in France to the Huns.

The Colonel and myself left by automobile on October 31st for the front. We were both unlucky and lucky. We were just entering Besancon when a French truck came through the gateway. We put on the brakes, but as it is a very steep grade and the roads were wet and slippery, we slid and crashed into the side of the great archway which serves as the gateway to the city. Fortunately, a General Headquarters car left Valdahon a few minutes after we did, and they picked us up and took us with them to Chaumont, which is General Pershing's Headquarters, or General Headquarters of the A.E.F. Here we stayed all night with some of our friends, and next morning continued on our way to Gondrecourt, which was the headquarters of our division—the First—and where the infantry had been stationed. Here we spent another night in billets. The next day Division Headquarters gave us a Cadillac and we proceeded to Sommervillers near Nancy, which was the headquarters of the Division at the front. We were assigned splendid billets in Dombasle and we settled down to make the most of our stay of ten days at the front.

Of course, we could now hear the boom of the guns at the front and we were beginning to realize there really was a war on. Also, in coming through Nancy we saw many evidences of the damage the Hun has done to that very pretty city by aero plane bombing—frightfulness, you know. Dombasle was also a favorite place with the Hun when it came to depositing bombs, but we escaped a "show" while we were there.

I neglected to say that aero-plane raids were quite frequent at Valdahon. Hardly a week passed there without at least one alarm, and a couple of times we saw some very pretty air battles in the vicinity of Besancon—not aero-plane against aero plane, but land anti-aircraft guns firing at the Boche planes. The air was simply filled with bursting shrapnel—little white puffs of smoke.

But to go on! On November 3rd, we went up to the real front to see the batteries, and during the next ten days we covered the entire front—about ten miles long—quite thoroughly, spending one day of it in the very front line at "les Jumelles" and "Arracourt", two strong points in the front line. We saw how thoroughly camouflaged the batteries were, and it really is wonderful. One could walk along at a distance and not realize a battery was within a hundred miles, when suddenly one would boom away not more than 500 or 600 yards away.

One crossroad we had to pass each day was a favorite target of the Hun, and at all sorts of odd times he would drop a few six-inch shells onto it. I must admit I was nervous the first couple of times I passed it, but it is surprising how soon it works off.

We travelled for miles in plain sight of the Boche lines, but even the roads were camouflaged so that he could not see us. And it was very simply done. The roads are all made of crushed limestone and so are white. A wide strip of white cloth is hung on posts along the side of the road toward the Hun, so that it appears and looks like the road, and yet the road is never occupied—at least, so far as the Hun can see.

Of course, before we ever went to the front, we were fitted out with gas masks, steel helmet, and so forth. The helmets are heavy things and ugly, but they are useful to a certain extent. We were all given two gas masks—one of the French type and one of the British type—but as we were not "gassed" while I was at the front, I can't say which is the better. But I can say that I believe I'd rather be "gassed" than wear one of them for any length of time, for they are hot, stuffy and exceedingly smelly. It is a horrible war when they even poison the air we breathe, isn't it? And one looks like a deep sea-diver, or some such thing, when wearing it. But "c'est la guerre," which is a common French expression of the day, meaning "It is the war."

While I was up, the first battalion finished its tour and the second battalion went into line. When we arrived things were quiet, but the Americans proceeded to make it interesting for the Hun and vice versa. Our infantry suffered several losses, and were raided once, this latter experience causing the 16th Infantry three killed, 8 wounded and 11 missing (carried off as prisoners by the Boche, of course.) It was too bad we could not have pulled the first raid, but we were entirely in French hands for instruction, and so were more or less helpless. Also, we cannot be blamed for the above raid—it wasn't our fault, and you can guess for yourself whose fault it was. The artillery escaped until the very last day with no losses, but on that day, after the 5th F.A. had pulled out their guns from their positions and were on the road home, a "crump" landed among them killing three men and wounding five. Hard luck, I would call it.

While at the front, we spent one day visiting a camouflage factory in Nancy. Its enormity can be imagined when I state the below figures. It employed 50 artists, 800 girls, and turned out 2000 meters of camouflage material per day. In addition to this camouflage material, which is simply canvas painted in ground colors or chicken wire in which is woven grass, it turns out observation posts or towers in the shape of trees, simple steel casks, etc., etc.

`On the day on which I visited the front-line trenches, I got my first taste of Hun "high life." The lines at this point are about 1800 yards apart, and we wandered around pretty much at will. We visited listening posts way out in No Man's Land, about 800 yards from the Hun lines, machine gun shelters and emplacements, dugouts, tunnels, etc., and all in all it was very interesting. It was after we had completed our rounds and were standing in a trench on the reverse slope of "les Jumelles'" which are a couple of twin hills over which the French trench runs, that fun began. Someone foolishly exposed themselves on top of the hill, and the Boche let go with six 41/2-inch shells, all of which fell within 50 yards of us. Fortunately, the ground was soft and we were somewhat protected by the crest of the hill, so that most of the fragments went straight up in the air, and we escaped with a splattering of mud. However, they were plenty close enough to be interesting.

The rest of our stay was quite uneventful and on Nov. 11th, we returned to Ribeaucourt, a small village in the Gondrecourt area, which was to be our home from now on instead of Valdahon. About a week later the second battalion returned from the front, and our work preparing for the winter and also more training work followed. Our billets were quite comfortable and clean, but awfully cold, for the French do not believe in warm homes. Also, they do not believe in fresh air, and when I insisted on opening my window every night, the old lady in whose house I was billeted nearly had a fit.

But I was not due to remain here long, for the Colonel recommended me to go to the General Staff College at Langres, as I was the senior captain in the regiment at the time. So, on Nov. 25th, I proceeded to Langres.

Langres was the site for the General Staff College established in France by order of General John Pershing. With the advent of hostilities in France, the Command and General Staff College at Fort Leavenworth was closed and the training of officers for higher staff assignments ceased. The rapid expansion of the Army required increasing numbers of staff officers. In an effort to meet that need, the General Staff College at Langres was established.

Langres is another old historical and fortified place. It is situated on a high lone hill, and is entirely surrounded with a stone wall and strong earth and stone fortifications. One of the gates was built by the Romans, and is still standing, but is no longer in use, having had the opening filled in with masonry. It is indeed an interesting old place, and has quite a history. It has withstood nearly, if not all, attempts to capture it in past centuries. In 1870 the Germans passed around it, as it was too hard a nut to crack.

Our course started on November 28th, and since then we have been busy studying and trying to keep ourselves warm, for the supply of fuel for our billets is very limited.

We had a couple of days off about December 16th, and Major Sherman and I ran up to Paris. We spent most of our time sightseeing, as we had only a day there. We strolled up the Champs Elysees, saw Eiffel Tower, the Arc de Triomphe, etc., etc. and in the evening, went to the Folies Bergere, a musical comedy. Paris is interesting and I hope to spend more time there before I return to the U.S.A.

Since then nothing of importance has happened here, but last Saturday our Division—the good old First—returned to the front and replaced the French division which acted as our instructors while we were at the front. So now we are really in the show, and I'm sure that, instead of that sector being a quiet one, as it has been heretofore, it will be very much alive from now on, like the British front is. I am an admirer of the British and their method of making it hot for the Hun all of the time, and I know we are going to be like them in that respect. Of course, all the men here who belong to the First Division wish they were there, but cheer up! We'll be with them shortly.

The month of January 1918 was spent in school at Langres, the Command and General Staff School established in France by General Pershing to train officers for higher staff duties. It was Pershing's hope to train sufficient numbers of officers in France for the waves of American doughboys bound for France.

Jan. 29th. We all went out to Fort d'Epigny where a battalion of infantry, and all the various schools such as Machine Gun, Stoke's

Mortar and Automatic Rifle schools, put on an imaginary attack on a German position. It was a splendid show—first the Machine Gun barrage fired over the heads of the infantry; then the Stokes Mortars and 37mm cannon came in with their heavier explosions. Suddenly the barrage ceased and our infantry went over the "top" and advanced to the first objective, whereupon the M.G.s, mortars, etc., increased their range and put the barrage down on the next objective. After a certain time, the barrage was again lifted and the infantry advanced to the attack of the second objective, and so on, until the final objective was reached. Cleaning-up parties bombed out the trenches with hand and rifle grenades; rockets, flares and smoke bombs were fired to show location of the infantry or to call for barrage, etc. and rifle grenades; rockets, flares and smoke bombs were fired to show location of the infantry or to call for barrage, etc., all of which was very realistic and very well pulled off. All it lacked was the Boche to fire back and make it hotter for our men. However, when the time comes for us to go against the real thing I know we'll do it exactly as successfully as those men did it today against imaginary Huns.

In the winter of 1917-1918, the Allies increased their efforts to coordinate training and doctrine with the expectation that American units would soon be fighting side by side with both the French and British armies.

Feb. 17th. Received order to proceed to Hdqrs. 22nd Corps of the British Army to complete my education as a staff officer. Left Chaumont at 5:00 p.m. and arrived in Paris at 10:00 p.m. Just as we arrived the "alerte" was sounded in Paris and all the street cars, subways, taxis and cabs stopped running and we were left high and dry at the station. The anti-aircraft guns started going and we spent a very noisy hour, but the Boche planes didn't get over Paris. Finally, I reached a hotel at 12:30.

Feb. 18th. Got up at 6:30 a.m., got my baggage stored and left Paris at 9:10 a.m. We travelled all day. The latter part of the day we passed numberless English camps. Also, it was this day that I first began to realize the enormous number of men who have met an untimely death in this war. Cemetery after cemetery, each one of which was simply a sea of crosses, was passed during the afternoon. I finally reached Calais at 5:00 p.m. and found it would be impossible to get forward that night. So, I put up at a hotel and spent the night there. And it was in Calais where I had my first real "bombing". Hun machines passed over at about 7:00 p.m. but did not molest us, as they were on their way to London. But only one machine succeeded in getting over London, so the remainder came back and dropped their cargos of bombs on Calais. I heard six bombs explode, but fortunately was several blocks from them at the time. The explosions, however, were terrific and quite terrifying. Also, the anti-aircraft kept up a noisy "show", which, combined with the explosion of the bombs, made an infernal noise. I really hope it will be the last raid I will be in, but I fear I'll have no such luck.

Feb. 19th. Proceeded to Abeele Station, a little village in Belgium, on this day and reported to the 22nd British Corps. Abeele is near Ypres—in fact this Corps holds the Ypres sector, which is indeed the hottest place along the whole front. We can hear the rumble of guns here, but otherwise live so comfortably that it is hard to realize we are at war and that the enemy is only 12 miles away. The officers here are splendid and mighty fine fellows and already I dislike the idea of leaving them. We have a squadron of aero planes here too, which are continually buzzing over us on their way over the German lines.

Captain Anderson's assertion that Ypres is "the hottest place along the whole front" was true. The Belgium town of Ypres is famous in the history of the Great War as the site of repeated assaults and counterattacks by the Germans and British. The Battle of the Somme in 1916 was a British attack that resulted in 54,470 casualties on the first day alone. In July 1917, the first Battle of Passchendaele signaled a prolonged campaign for control of the ridges south and east of Ypres, the high ground that commanded the area. The battle continued on and off until November 1917, when rain, mud, and exhaustion stopped the assault. The British suffered more than 200,000 casualties in this battle of attrition and gained a total of eight kilometers in the campaign. The futility of the back and forth combat is illustrated in a comment by a Canadian officer who arrived at the front in October 1917 in the same location occupied by his unit in 1915.[6] The despair of the British Tommies was captured in part by the British war poet Siegfried Sassoon who wrote, "I died in Hell. They called it Passchendaele."

In the winter and early spring of 1918, the British held Ypres.

Feb. 20th. Went out to the airdrome today and met a lot of the aviators. They are a fine bunch of fellows. Also, their attitude is interesting. A pilot and his observer start off with a smile and a wave of the hand to everyone, and seem to think nothing of their dangerous mission. When they return no one pays them much attention but take it as a matter of course that they are back. Two of them dined with us this evening and very interesting they were too.

Feb. 21st. I dined with Lieut. General Godley,[7] the Corps Commander, this evening. He has visited the U.S. and inspected the Corps of Cadets in the fall of 1910 while I was a cadet. Unfortunately, I could not remember the occasion.

Feb. 22nd. Dined with the aviation fellows today, and it was a very interesting luncheon too. We had two Hun prisoners this morning. They seemed to be quite well fed and healthy. The Intelligence Officer tried to get information from them, but they either knew nothing or else knew a lot which they were not at all inclined to tell. Of course, he succeeded in getting a little information from them about trenches, Machine Gun emplacements, etc., most of which, however, he knew before. Yesterday I had an example of what a science modern warfare is. About ten o'clock in the morning a telephone message came in from a listening post saying they had overheard a message sent by an enemy observation post to an enemy battery to open fire on a British working party on a certain road. The message was immediately telephoned to Division Headquarters of the New Zealand Division, which is in the line, and the party notified to take cover. Later I learned that the working party got under cover before the Hun opened fire on them. These listening posts are quite wonderful. Of course, it is no trick to pick up wireless messages, but it is quite a trick to pick up telephone messages, especially metallic circuit telephones. But it is done by a simple little instrument called a listening-in set, and as a result very valuable information is obtained. Both sides use it, of course, which has necessitated the use of codes for all extremely important messages.

Feb. 24th. Some fighting planes came down today to give us a demonstration air-fight. It was excellent, and the stunts they pulled off in the air were marvelous. After the "show", I went up for a short flight with one of the youngsters of the squadron here in a two-seater reconnaissance plane. We flew to Ypres and almost to the front line, but did not cross "No Man's Land" as we were not prepared to fight with any Hun scout plane who happened along.

Feb. 25th. It rained this morning but in spite of the weather we went up to the front. The ruin and destruction beg description, but the aero plane photographs I have will give a slight idea of what it is like. The mud and water are awful, and the roads full of holes, shell holes, and mud. About the only way trucks and wagons can move are over the corduroy roads, which are built all over the area. Board sidewalks cover the country and also are placed in all trenches, for otherwise it would be very nearly impossible for one on foot to move. The waste and destruction of war never came home to me so forcibly as it did today. Villages, nothing but heaps of dirt, bricks and rubbish; cities razed to the ground; forests destroyed entirely, with nothing but a few stumps or shattered tree trunks to show where they had been, and the whole country-side one mass of shell-holes so close together it is impossible to find tracks between them—in fact, the shell-holes meet each other. And through it all the human races—the British here—carry on. It is a good example of the bull dog tenacity of the British—to say nothing of the doggedness of the Hun—that he, or both, have not stopped long ago. The men are wonderful to go on under the circumstances, living day in and day out in mud and water up to their waists, being shelled constantly and with freezing weather continually. Even the dugouts are full of water and none too comfortable a place. And to top it all off, the Boche sends over a nice little package of gas every day, or even several times a day. Let us hope our men will show the same splendid fighting spirit, and, of course, we know they will. While we were up, the enemy was remarkably quiet, though we did get a half a dozen or more shells a few hundred yards away.

Feb. 28th. Moved up to Heavy Artillery Headquarters for a couple of days stay today. This brings me right into the midst of things, and I am getting a little taste of what it is like to live in a house of sandbags, steel, etc., which is put down in the ground and called a dugout. But I am quite comfortable, for we are on a slight hill and much drier than most of the poor devils are in their holes. It has been quite quiet this afternoon up here. The air has been full of our planes and Hun planes and the anti-aircraft guns (Archie's, we call them) have been popping away at a great pace at them, but so far none have been hit. Also, there were no air fights between planes. The Boche started firing on one of our balloons late in the afternoon, and though he came close, he failed to hit it. However, he forced it to descend. This evening there has been quite a heavy bombardment north of us, and the sky is one mass of light.

March 1. March came in today like a lion in more ways than one. It has turned much colder, and has snowed off and on all day. We went around to see the Flash-Spotting and Sound-Ranging Stations this afternoon. They are quite wonderful and do exceedingly accurate and excellent work. Their methods are quite simple, but too long to describe. Their purpose, of course, is to locate the position of Hun batteries by intersection of lines from various stations seeing the flash of his guns, which is flash-spotting, or by means of intersection of lines of sound, which is done by a very delicate and intricate mechanism which photographs the vibrations of spider web strings caused by the explosion of the gun. It is truly wonderful. I also visited a wireless station yesterday, and they locate Hun wireless stations in much the same manner. Various stations catch his messages, and by means of tuning, etc., they can tell from which direction the message comes. By intersection of these lines, the enemy wireless station is located. The day, with a little intermittent shelling, was very quiet, but this evening the fun started at about 7 o'clock and continued until 11 o'clock. Several S.O.S. signals were sent up by our infantry, and immediately all our guns opened up on various Boche batteries, roads and trenches. The sky was one blaze of fire—like a severe lightning storm, and the noise was deafening. Altogether, six S.O.S.'s were sent up by our infantry, so the bombardment was more or less continuous. What really happened was that the Boche was trying to raid our lines to get prisoners for information purposes. As soon as the enemy is seen concentrating in his trenches or gets into No Man's Land, our infantry sends up an S.O.S. signal rocket and down comes our barrage on the Hun trenches and batteries. Of course, the Hun also protects his raiding parties by means of barrages and fire on our batteries, back areas, headquarters, etc., so that it is rather lively for us all. All his raiding attempts failed in the early part of the night, but early the morning of the 2nd he finally got across but was "strafed" by our infantry, had several killed and wounded, and finally had to retire without taking a prisoner, but leaving three in our hands. This brings the total number of prisoners captured by the Corps the two weeks I have been here up to 25.

March 3. Am getting ready to leave tomorrow for the 1st Division. Today has been cold and wet, so we've not done much. Saw an English football match today.

Mar. 4. After saying goodbye to Capt. Calthrop, Lieut. Huddleston, Lieut. Costello, Capt. Hanson, Capt. Elliott, and others of the British Army, I left Abeele at 8:30 this morning. I arrived at Calais at 11:30, then proceeded to Boulogne, arriving there at 1:30. At 2:10 I boarded the Paris train, arriving in Paris at 8:30 P.M. Went to the Hotel de Crillon, where I met several friends.

Wartime is said to be a time of rushed friendships and comradery. Anderson was sorry to leave these officers even though—or maybe because—they were Englishmen. He knew the history of the war and that their days might be numbered and wished to memorialize them in his own small way by listing their names and ranks in his diary.

Mar. 8. Spent a long day in Toul waiting for a car to come and take us to our division headquarters. It finally arrived at 3:00 p.m. and we arrived at Division Headquarters at 4:00 p.m. I reported to the Chief of Staff and was assigned to the 1st F.A. Brigade as adjutant. I reported to Brig. Gen. Summerall,[8] who commands the Brigade, and immediately got to work. In the evening, the Hun planes flew over us and our anti-aircraft guns got busy. Three times they crossed us, but fortunately for us, they dropped no bombs.

Mar. 9. Working hard. Beautiful weather today. The Hun brought down a French plane within our lines this afternoon in an air fight.

General Pershing and General Summerall, Spring, 1918

Mar. 10. My birthday today. Can't say that I feel much older for having passed another milestone. Nothing of especial importance, except that I took a trip up to the forward positions today. A few stray shots, but everything more or less quiet. Beautiful weather.

On this date, Captain Anderson, in his role as acting adjutant, promulgated the following:

HEADQUARTERS FIRST FIELD ARTILLERY BRIGADE
AMERICAN EXPEDITIONARY FORCES
General Orders. No. 4

- It becomes the privilege and proud duty of the Brigade Commander to communicate the following letter to the First Field Artillery Brigade:

  From: Division Commander
  To: General C.P. Summerall, Commanding 1st Artillery Brigade
  Subject: Action of Artillery Brigade in REMIERES and RICHECOURT Raids, March 11, 1918

  I wish to express to you and to the officers and men of your command my appreciation of the efficiency of the fire of your guns that has enabled the raiding detachments to perform their missions without interference by the enemy and without loss of a man, and has undoubtedly inflicted heavy losses on the enemy in addition to destroying his fortifications.

The infantry has been inspired with a great confidence by the assurance of instant and effective support by the Artillery.

Please communicate my congratulations to your command.

Major General R.L. Bullard

• The Brigade Commander desires to add his profound appreciation of the efficiency of the services and the high order of duty to which the division commander has so generously testified. In acquitting itself of the grave responsibilities that have rested upon it in establishing a standard for the action of Artillery during the formative period of our greatly augmented forces, this Brigade has vindicated the methods of discipline, training and soldierly deportment that have been exacted throughout the command. By continuation of these virtues and by earnestness of purpose and devoted zeal on the part of officers and men, the Brigade will enhance its reputation and will add new standards to the traditions of the Army.

• This Order will be read to every battery, company and detachment of the Brigade within six hours after its receipt at each place.

By command of Brigadier General Summerall:
John B. Anderson, Captain, 6th F.A., Acting Adjutant

After his time at headquarters as acting adjutant to General Summerall, Anderson was dispatched to the front to replace the commanding officer of the Second Battalion, incapacitated by a German gas attack.

Mar. 12. The commanding officer of the 2nd Battalion, 6th F.A., and all the officers and men of Battery D were overcome by German gas last night, and were sent to the hospital. So, I was sent up by the General today to take temporary command of the 2nd Battalion—a major's job. I have spent the whole day going into the "gassed" dugouts, with a mask on, or course, rescuing papers, maps, etc. Also, have gotten my officers together, gotten new men and officers to man "D" Battery and in general have been exceedingly busy. I now have three batteries to look after, and as they are in pretty well scattered positions, it is quite a job visiting them. I had to move "D" Battery to a new position on account of the gas, but hope to send them back soon. Hun and French planes, Hun and American balloons were up all-day taking advantage of the beautiful weather.

Captain Anderson was now in combat in command of the Second Battalion, Sixth Field Artillery Regiment. His appointment reflects the realities of war and the unexpected nature of casualties.

Mar. 13. Inspected my batteries nearly all day, including Observation Posts. It was very quiet along the front today, except this evening when they shot up the crossroad not more than 100 yards from my dugout. Two men from "F" Battery, who were hauling supplies, were killed; two wounded and two horses killed. Planes and balloons quite active. The anti-aircraft guns pop away continually but never seem to hit a plane. It is very pretty to watch the puffs of smoke of the bursts follow the plane around. The fragments from the shells are very dangerous to us, however, as I can bear witness after having had a large piece of one fall alongside of me today. The crossroads I mentioned are a favorite target of the Huns, and many of the strays fall near my happy home. One lit on it one day, but didn't hurt it or go through, so I feel more or less safe there.

Mar. 17. A beautiful day. Quiet all day except our anti-aircraft guns brought down a Hun plane within our lines—at last. It was a welcome sight too. A Frenchman was forced to land in our lines yesterday as the Hun anti-aircraft shot a piece of his engine away. He made a safe landing, however, and no damage was done to his machine except the part which had been shot away. At six o'clock this evening the Hun opened a "Hymn of Hate" on two of my battery positions. One of them was unoccupied, thank heavens, so the only damage done was that some of the camouflage caught fire and burned up. Poor old "D" Battery was in the other position, and caught it hard. One gun was knocked out, a lot of ammunition exploded, part of the camouflage burnt up, and two men were wounded. The whole position was surrounded with shell holes, but fortunately none of the shells hit vital spots except the one above-mentioned. Six-inch shells were the dose, and they were coming at the rate of 5 or 6 a minute for about an hour. Just a little St. Patrick's Day fun, I suppose.

Mar. 18. Spent all day with the different batteries. One French plane and two Hun planes had a fight, but the Frenchman had to leave. Mighty interesting. Our anti-aircraft guns drove the Huns back home. I spent the afternoon at one of my observation stations hoping the Hun balloons would go down so I could adjust my batteries on a new barrage, but he was too persistent. During the afternoon, he amused himself by firing into the woods in which we were, and we were kept busy dodging nasty, whining pieces of shell. This evening we had a gas alarm, but there wasn't enough of it to be dangerous.

Mar. 19. A beautiful day and of course there was a great deal of air activity. The shelling on both sides was more or less intermittent and weak. Secretary of War Baker arrived at about 5 o'clock in the afternoon and inspected some of the trenches and batteries. He didn't stay long however.

It was during Secretary Baker's inspection trip that the Germans launched their spring offensive. He heard and witnessed the crescendo of German artillery fire during a visit to a First Division hospital.

The Ludendorff Offensive, the Kaiser's Battle, and Operation Michael are names given to the German spring offensive of 1918, the last offensive effort of Germany to win the war. On the first day of the assault, the British gave up all the territory near Ypres taken during the three-and-a-half-month Passchendaele campaign of 1917.

Mar. 21st. Our wireless report today reported active artillery engagements farther north. I wonder if the German much talked of offensive is near. Everything is quiet here, except a few points which were attacked with gas shell. My batteries sent back two or three shells for every one the Fritz put in our territory however. Artillery duels still continue farther north this evening.

Mar. 22. Clear and beautiful weather again today, which always brings out the planes. More gas from the other side today, but we sent back a lot. I turned my batteries loose this afternoon and am doing so again tonight and tomorrow morning. We'll feed the beggars up on their own medicine if they so wish. Artillery still reported active up north.

Mar. 23. The German drive is on and from all reports everything is looking black for the allies. But they'll never break through us—instead they will use up their men and materials which will make it easier for us to crush them to earth and win the final great and decisive victory. Very quiet in this sector. Beautiful weather. Enormous gun reported firing on Paris. It is inconceivable and I can't believe it.

Mar. 24. We still are receiving discouraging reports from the north. But the British will stop them, of that I am certain. Rumor about gun firing on Paris has been confirmed. Range—75 miles. It is hard to believe. Usual air activity and artillery duels here. One of my guns was knocked out by enemy fire last night. Today I had a rather novel experience. It is not novel to us here for it happens every day, but to those who have never been on the Western Front it may seem strange. So here it is. I stood out in the open and watched Fritz firing on a trench with shell 500 yards away; also watched our own and enemy planes flying about overhead. And I was quite safe. And so, it is always. Unless you happen to be at the spot on which old Fritz decides to wreak vengeance you are quite safe anywhere along the front. It is the chance shot which gets you. This is true during ordinary quiet times, and is quite untrue during an attack, such as is going on to the north of us now.

Mar. 27. Last night about 11:00 o'clock the normal barrage rocket was sent up by the infantry. We immediately put down the barrage and stopped whatever the German was trying to do. Of course, when our artillery opened up, the Hun artillery started also, and things were popping for about 50 minutes. The sky was a blaze of light all along the front as far as we could see. Still not much news from the north except that the fighting which is very desperate on both sides, continues.

March 28. All calm here today. A beautiful day for flying and a good many planes were up, with the usual anti-aircraft shooting. At nine o'clock this evening heavy enemy firing was reported on our front, and immediately I ordered my batteries to fire in barrage. Soon things were going at a great rate—not only our artillery but the Hun's as well. He gave us a dose of something new last night—liquid fire. A lot of our batteries had their camouflage catch on fire, but no one was much harmed by the fire. He then followed with the usual gas—phosgene and mustard gas. Four out of six of my battery positions were filled with gas, and the men had to continue the fire with their masks on, which is far from pleasant. Two officers and seven men from my batteries had to be sent to the hospital as a result of the gas. I got a good whiff myself but not enough to more than make me momentarily dizzy. A very strong wind blew the gas away so rapidly that our casualties were very much less than they would have been had it been a quiet night. Of course, we got a lot of high explosive shell along with the flame and gas but it didn't reach any vital spots, except my telephone wires, all of which were cut. The heavy firing kept up for about one- and one-half hours and then slowed up, but the whole night was more or less busy. This is only an echo; however, compared with what is doing up north. The "show" here has a beautiful sight, the entire heavens being lit up by the flash of the guns and the fires.

Mar. 29. This morning our infantry patrols went over into Hunland and ran into ten Huns. Four were killed, four were brought back prisoners and two escaped. They came back home over No Man's Land in broad daylight. Rather good work, I would say. My batteries have been doing a little sniping the past two days. We have been firing at working parties, wagons, etc., which the men enjoy very much, even though they don't see their target, for only the officer in the Observation Post can see them. It rained this morning, and all in all is quite disagreeable. Reports from the north say the Hun advance has been checked completely. I certainly hope it is true.

The diary stops here. In the first week of April 1918, the First Division moved from Toul to the area of Cantigny. This area was near the junction of the British and French armies, which was the target of the Germans in their spring offensive.

The German offensive began with seventy-six divisions of the German Army attacking the Allied front where the British Fifth Army adjoined the French Sixth Army east of Amiens. As the Germans drove nearly twenty miles across a fifty-mile front toward Amiens, there was a real chance that the Germans would cut the railroad communications between the British and the French.

General Philippe Petain, commander-in-chief of the French Army, requested that General Pershing move the US Army's First Division to Picardy, northwest of Paris, to the area of greatest danger, the area where the main battle was raging. On the evening of April 4, the First Division's infantry boarded fifty-seven troop trains and assembled over the next two days near Chaumont-en-Vexin and Gisors. The operation was conducted in large part by George Marshall and Campbell King, owing to the absence of the division's commanding officer General Bullard, hospitalized in Toul. The supply trains, including the sanitation, ammunition, and medical units, came by motor vehicle columns and horse-drawn wagons; the supply trains and the infantry were joined on April 12.

Pershing visited on April 16 and spoke to the First Division's officers near Chaumont-en-Vexin. He expressed his confidence that the division would maintain its excellent record achieved during its training and previous fighting. It is said that "The General threw the whole of his forceful personality into this short talk; every officer was inspired to do his best out of personal loyalty to such a chief, even if for no other motive."

On April 17, the First Division became part of the French First Army, under their strategic but not tactical control. First Infantry Brigade troops moved into the line on the night of April 24-25 with the Eighteenth Infantry Regiment on the north and the Sixteenth Infantry Regiment to the south.

There was much fighting left for the American Expeditionary Force between May and November 1918 including the Battles of Cantigny, Belleau Wood, Chateau Thierry, Soisson, and St. Mihiel. However, the war was over for Captain Anderson. On May 15, 1918, he was ordered back to Washington to the Army War College. He objected to this transfer. His immediate commanding officer, Brigadier General Summerall, the commanding general of the First Brigade Artillery, supported his effort to remain in France, but Summerall was overruled by Major General Bullard, the commanding general of the First Division. Bullard was acting on Pershing's orders to find officers capable of training the next wave of officers and men for duty in France. Pershing had concluded that training facilities in France were inadequate and that training would need to occur in the United States prior to deployment overseas to France. Officers like Captain Anderson were deemed more important to the war effort preparing the next wave of men heading to France than continued service at the front.

Anderson returned to the United States and took leave to visit his home. On June 18, 1918, he gave a talk to the local townspeople of Parkersburg at the Methodist Church, the largest building available. An account of the event was published in the local newspaper.

Captain Anderson with nephew Jack Richardson, Parksburg, 1918

"One of the largest audiences ever gathered in the Methodist Church assembled last Sunday night to hear Captain J.B. Anderson speak on phases of the war, a subject he is well fitted to talk about after an experience of ten months with the American Expeditionary forces in France. At 7:30 the crowd began to assemble at the church, and by the time the hour for services arrived every available seat in the big auditorium, Sunday School room, and the gallery was occupied by a throng eager to pay tribute to a Parkersburg boy who has made good, and is climbing rapidly in the military circles. Capt. Anderson is a graduate of West Point, has seen service in the regular army on the Mexican border, and was one of the first of the troops sent to France. He is sent back to America to take a place on the general military staff at

Washington. He has been recommended for advancement to the rank of major, and will within a very short time be wearing the insignia of that honorable office.

"The Captain spoke of the scientific methods of warfare as now in use. He gave a vivid description of 'No Man's Land' and of various tactics employed in preparing for and taking trenches.

"He demonstrated the use of the gas mask, having with him one of the French and one of the English masks.

"He also had his metal helmet—'not a thing of adornment, but extremely useful in guarding the head against injury from shrapnel or other light missiles.'

"At the end of his address he gave the audience permission to ask questions and much interesting information was given in his answers. He stated that by July first we will have a million men in France, and that it takes four men to keep one man at the front fighting; so that a million would mean but 250,000 available for actual fighting.

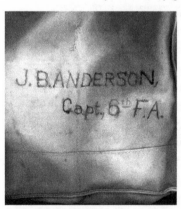

Captain Anderson's gask mask, 1918

"The Captain left Monday evening for Chicago for a couple of days visit with his sister before going on to Washington to assume his duties.

"The Congregational church adjourned their services to unite with the big meeting at the Methodist church and many were present from the other churches and a host from the country round about. The size of the congregation and the enthusiastic spirit manifested, speaks well for the patriotic spirit of the community."

What a heady experience for the returning twenty-seven-year-old warrior! To come home to the people with whom he had grown up, to have survived the horror of the Western Front, and to bask in the adoration of friends and family vindicated his decision eight years before to attend West Point. He had kept his nose clean and studied hard during his four years to graduate in the upper third of his class. He had gone off to the heat and dust of the Texas border and impressed Pershing and his staff well enough to be selected to go to France with the men who fired the first rounds into the German lines. And now, he was selected to come home to train the next wave of soldiers heading to France. From the moments of great excitement of listening to the singing of "The Marseillaise" and "Tipperary" at St. Nazaire, to the time when he crashed his motorcycle in a manure pile, and to his survival of a gas attack in Flanders, he had participated in and witnessed many important events in the course of the early war years. To have seen the horrors of war, to have experienced the intensity of combat, to have witnessed the deaths of comrades and soldiers under his command, and to have returned home alive and well confirmed his choice to cast his lot with the Army.

Amid his excitement and pride, he knew his life in Parkersburg was over. His brother Nels was absent, living in San Francisco. His mother and father were dead and buried in his absence. His niece Louisa had been stricken with polio. Parkersburg was not the same town he left in 1910. After this June 1918 visit, he never returned. He attended none of the funerals of his family, from his aunt Amelia Simonsen in the 1930s to his sister Margaret in 1971. The lure of military glory, the demands of service, and the distance home were too great.

CHAPTER 5

AFTER THE WAR TO END ALL WARS

1918-1941

A fter his visit to Parkersburg in June 1918, Captain Anderson reported to the Historical Section of the Army War College in Washington. On July 17, he was promoted to major of field artillery in the Army.

Major Anderson's promotion certificate, 1918

His report to the Historical Section of the Army War College completed, he transferred to the Firing Center at Fort Sill, Oklahoma, the home of advanced field artillery training. The rapid expansion of the Army was continuing, and more experienced senior officers were needed. In September 1918, Major Anderson was promoted again, this time to the temporary rank of lieutenant colonel. The pace of promotion was intoxicating.

And then the war was over, at eleven a.m. on November 11. The need for training of officers in the techniques and tactics of field artillery evaporated. He was reassigned, this time to the Office of the Chief of Field Artillery in Washington.

Lieutenant Colonel Anderson was twenty-seven years old, living as a guest in the home of Colonel William H. Dodds, and divorced. He wondered what the future held.

The Army demobilized and its ranks contracted severely under the congressional mandates of the 1920 National Defense Act. Although this legislation purported to guarantee readiness by expanding opportunities for National Guard officers alongside regular Army officers, in fact the legislation left the United States woefully unprepared for war.

Lieutenant Colonel Anderson Portrait, 1920

On July 1, 1920, Lieutenant Colonel Anderson reverted to the permanent rank of major. The rank of lieutenant colonel would not be his again until 1935.

The life of an eligible bachelor from rural Iowa in Washington, DC, in the 1920s was very different than life in Parkersburg or El Paso. Washington was a "Southern" town that valued good manners and civility. As a West Point graduate, and an officer and a gentleman, doors were opened to Major Anderson. On February 23, 1922, he dined at the White House by invitation of President and Mrs. Harding.

His assignment in Washington at the Office of the Chief of Field Artillery lasted almost four years. After a short stint in the advanced course of the Field Artillery School at Fort Sill, Oklahoma, Major Anderson assumed command of the Eighty-third Field Artillery at Fort Benning in Columbus, Georgia. Fort Benning was the site of the US Army Advanced Infantry School. The school was established through the efforts of local citizen groups led by George C. Palmer, a prominent Columbus attorney.

Fort Benning is named for Columbus native Henry L. Benning, one of the staunchest states' rights advocates of the South who

83rd FIELD ARTILLERY

FLAGRANTE BELLO

Eighty-Third Field Artillery Badge, 1924

served "The Cause" as a brigadier general of the Confederate States Army. He was described as "one of nature's noblemen formed in her finest mould and most lavish prodigality. As an attorney, he was open, candid, and fair; as a jurist, spotless and impartial; as a warrior and patriot, brave, disinterested, and sincere; as a man and citizen, his whole life produced in those who knew him, the constant vibration of those chords which answer to all that is true and noble, generous, and manly."[9]

The Infantry School at Fort Benning is dedicated to the memory of those fallen comrades, doughboys, resting forever in France. The motto of the Infantry School is "Follow me."

Citizens wanted the officers at Fort Benning to feel welcome. *The Doughboy* is the yearbook of the Infantry School, and in 1924 it described Columbus as "a hospitable town, anxious to cement its relationship with the U.S. Army, opening its figurative arms to the young officers assigned to the Infantry School."

Caisson Ride Fort Benning, April 24, 1924

Major Anderson took advantage of the charms of the city. In the autumn of 1923, he met, courted, and won the hand of Sue Moore Palmer, the only daughter of Attorney George C. Palmer, the very same Georgian who had lobbied so successfully for the selection of Columbus as an Army training camp.

The major and Miss Palmer were married on April 24, 1924, and took the proverbial "caisson ride" around the dusty parade grounds of the Infantry School. Years later, Sue Palmer Anderson was to recall that, despite the swirling dust that covered her dainty white gown and hat, she was "all smiles."

The next assignment for Major Anderson was the Command and General Staff School at Fort Leavenworth, Kansas. In late 1924, he and his new wife headed to the Midwest. Mrs. Anderson was pregnant with the couple's first and only child. Shortly after their arrival in Kansas, their daughter, Sue Moore Anderson, was born on January 14, 1925.

The Command and General Staff School at Fort Leavenworth is an important stepping-stone for all Army officers. The principles of high command and the methods of handling larger combats units are taught in a highly competitive academic environment. The foundation of instruction was "application exercises," formal solutions to increasingly complex problems. Although the solutions were the result of committees of students, the students were graded individually. Students were required to use the proper order and messaging formats to communicate their decisions and hypothetical orders. These formats distinguished Command and General Staff College graduates in later years.

Lectures were rigorously prepared prior to presentation to student officers. Lectures and conferences complemented the "committee" work; conferences were ungraded audience participation events, not rote presentations. Terrain problems were added and consisted of open-air exercises on horseback at Fort Leavenworth or the surrounding countryside.

As the year progressed, problems of increasing complexity in combined arms at the division and corps levels taxed the students' stamina, intellect, and physical endurance. Grading of individuals' performance increased to two or three times a week. Major Anderson graduated with honors in 1925, ranking twentieth out of the 258 members of his class.

At the completion of the one-year-long course, the couple and their one-and-a-half-year-old daughter sailed to the Philippines for his father's second overseas assignment, this one for two years with the Twenty-fourth Field Artillery at Fort Stotsenburg, fifty miles north of Manila.

While overseas, Major Anderson wrote letters to his "adopted" parents, Mr. and Mrs. Palmer, aka "mother and daddy."

February 26, 1926
Camp Stotsenburg, Philippines

Dearest mother and daddy:

My brand of stationery is nothing to be proud of, but I hope you will overlook it as I am writing this in my office and this is all that I have available.

I spent last week at the Army and Navy joint maneuvers at Corregidor as an observer. The Navy were the enemy and the Coast Artillery, assisted by some infantry from the mainland, were the defending force. The Air Service was divided up, part operating with the "enemy" and part with the defending force. The enemy were trying to capture Manila Bay and Manila.

Corregidor lies at the entrance to Manila Bay and about 30 miles west of Manila. It is an island about two miles wide and four miles long, and rises almost perpendicularly out of the water to a height of 600 feet. It is heavily fortified, being rated even stronger than Gibraltar. The entire defense scheme at the mouth of the Bay involves Corregidor and three other smaller islands, all fortified with very heavy guns. However, at the present time we are limited by the disarmament conference agreements and no additional armament can be placed on the islands. Japan, you will remember, succeeded in putting across a clause in the Washington conference agreements that no additional fortifications or armament would be placed on any islands in the western Pacific. In other words, we lost out, and Japan got just what she wanted, for she had already fortified everything she wanted to fortify to the full limit. Furthermore, Japan is probably violating the agreement if she sees fit to do so or if she feels it to be to her advantage to do so, while we are religiously living up to it. But after all this digression, I will say I enjoyed the trip and was glad to be able to see the fortifications and also the maneuvers.

I ordered some pictures which a friend of mine took on a hunting expedition he went on last week up in the mountains about seven miles from here. They shot a 21-foot python and three deer while away. The pictures also show the Negritos, the uncivilized, short statured tribes that live in the hills around here. They come on the post frequently to sell air plants and most of them are quite harmless. They wear few clothes and depend on bows and arrows, bolos and crude spears for their hunting weapons. The pictures are not finished yet but I'll send them in the very near future.

Our hot season has begun but while the days are excessively hot, the nights are cool. The old-timers here tell me that the nights are always cool, no matter how hot the day. Also, I do not feel or mind the heat over here the way one does in the states, probably because our blood thins out and we become somewhat accustomed to it. But there is no doubt but what Kansas heat, Georgia heat and all summer heat at home is far harder to stand than this heat over here. We expect to go to Baguio about April 15 and remain at least a month. That will be the hottest period of the year as the rainy season begins about June 15th and from then until Nov. 1st, it is quite cool. The heavy rains make everything damp, musty and moldy, but if it is cool we can't complain about the dampness.

The old "Thomas"[10] is again here and leaves Saturday for the States. This makes her second visit here since our arrival, and now only six or seven more before we will again board her for home. And we'll all be glad when that time arrives. At present Sue and I are again contemplating a return by way of Suez and Europe, but our financial condition a year from now will of course be the guiding factor in that decision.

Sue and little Sue are well and happy. Little Tudy is walking—attempting to do so—and talking all the time. Her vocabulary is increasing rapidly and her enunciation is also clearer day by day. She is crazy to walk and keeps us all working leading her by the hand while she walks around the house. If you hold her in your lap she at once begins to pull and squirm in her attempts to get on the floor and says "wa-wa", meaning walk. I wish you could all see her again, and likewise I wish we could see you all again.

The pictures of George and Martie are splendid and we surely appreciate them. Isabel and Duff surely have good reason to be proud of such handsome and splendid specimens of childhood.[11]

Write us often for we live from mail boat to mail boat and the letters they bring us from you. Love to you all at home from us all.

As ever, Andy

P.S. Sue's and my golf are rapidly improving. Sue is an enthusiast. Also, she is down to 134 pounds as a result of the exercise.   A.

Sue Palmer Anderson

Upon completion of duties with the Twenty-fourth Field Artillery in the Philippines, Major Anderson was ordered back to Washington to the Army War College in 1927.

The family returned to the United States in 1927 via San Francisco. They visited his brother Nels, who was still living there. This is the last time the two Anderson brothers would see each other.

Back in Washington, Major Anderson joined the Army War College Class of 1927-1928. Several members of this class would go on to have storied military careers, including Dwight Eisenhower and Joseph Stillwell. Another member of the class was William H. Simpson, USMA 1909, who would become John Anderson's great friend and commanding officer in World War II.

Major Anderson completed his Army War College course and returned to the War Department General Staff. While on the staff, he was appointed a technical advisor to the American delegation to the 1929 Geneva Convention of the Treatment of War Prisoners. Hugh R. Wilson, American Minister to Switzerland and Eliot Wadsworth, former Assistant Secretary of the Treasury, headed the US delegation. The convention was held to revise the Geneva Convention of 1906 to draft rules for the treatment of prisoners of war and belligerent wounded. The hope of the signatory nations was to mitigate the horrors of war.

Geneva Convention Delegate Hall, 1929
Major Anderson is in the front row in tan civilian suit.

George Buck Tudy, 1929

Major Anderson and his wife, along with their dog, Donnie, lived in Geneva during his participation in the conference. Their four-year old daughter, Sue, nicknamed "Tudy," stayed in the United States, living with her grandparents Eva and George C. Palmer in Columbus, Georgia.

Anderson's postcards to "mother and daddy" reveal little of the life of a convention delegate beyond social events and sight-seeing.

July 12, 1929
Geneva, Switzerland

Dear mother and daddy:

We are lonesome for Tudy, but otherwise are enjoying the beautiful weather and scenery here in Geneva. Expect to finish my work here about the 25th, and will then return to Paris and from there to London and such other side trips as we may decide to take if time permits. Love to you both, Tudy, Duff, and his family.

As ever, Andy

The Geneva Convention concluded in the early summer of 1929. To the present day, the rules adopted govern the treatment of prisoners of war and wounded belligerents.

The next card from Anderson reveals that they also traveled with a personal servant named Mamie.

July 25, 1929
Geneva, Switzerland

Dear mother, daddy, and Tudy:

Sue and Mamie are in Paris, and I am joining them there on the 31st, when we will have finished our work here. Mamie and I went up to the ice fields shown on the reverse side, but Sue couldn't go. It was worthwhile. Love to you all at home, and some kisses for that Tudy.

As ever, Andy

July 28, 1929
Geneva, Switzerland

Dear mother and daddy:

We finished up our work at the Conference yesterday, signed the conventions, and I am now en route to Paris, by way of the Rhine, to meet Sue. I am so lonesome, however, for Sue that I am not enjoying the trip, and I would throw it overboard and go straight to Paris if that were now possible. However, I'll arrive there the 31st, and mighty glad of it.

Love, Andy

Prior to departure, Anderson visited Coblenz, Germany, the site on the Rhine River where the Sixth Field Artillery Regiment and the First Division crossed into Germany at the end of the World War.

July 30, 1929
Coblenz, Germany

Dearest mother and daddy:

The beauty of the trip up the Rhine this morning begs description. It was marred by the fact that Sue and you all couldn't or wouldn't, be with me to enjoy it. I hope someday to repeat it with all of you. The Lordey and its winds and echoes are really wonderful.

Love, Andy. I join Sue in
Paris tomorrow.

Upon his return to Washington, Anderson rejoined the War Department General Staff. Now almost forty years old, he corresponded with his older brother about his heritage and family history in Denmark.

Nels Anderson wrote from San Francisco the following letter to his brother:

November 15, 1930
218 12th Avenue, San Francisco, California

Dear brother:

I can't give you much encouragement in the ancestry line. When I received my commission in 1900 mother sent one of my photos to her sister at the Danish court. The letter acknowledging same bore a crest or coat-of-arms, but that may have belonged to the husband. I can't even recall their name now. There was some further correspondence.

All that I had collected on the subject went up in the S.F. earthquake[12] and fire. But here are a few facts from a more or less imperfect memory. The estate that went out of mother's family on the death of her father was called Aarhus. Her father was named Simonsen, was privy counselor to King Christian IX, and a legislator in the lower house. His wife's brother was Governor Finsen of Iceland. Niels Finsen, the discoverer of violet rays for cure of lupus, was his son. Your great-grandmother on mother's side was a Diemann, and going back from her are various literati, sculptors and professional men and women, and nobility. Father's people seem to have been on the sturdy yeomanry, and land-owning bourgeoisie.

I know of no member of mother's family (brothers and sisters) who are alive today, unless it is the aunt lady-in waiting and an uncle in Australia. Three of her brothers seem to have been sea captains, and were all lost at sea. The brother in Australia appears to be wealthy, and has a very large family.

After the destruction of records, I had collected, I took little further interest in these matters. It was only because we were required to have an ancestral background to get by in our examinations from the ranks in those days that I ever troubled about it. To me it all seems so futile. Especially so after actively interesting myself in church affairs.

Your suggestion that I see different doctors is of course sound. I had already done so, at the time you wrote from Margaret's. Three agree pretty closely, and they diagnose my case as hypertension, weakened heart muscles and leaky valves. They prescribe digitalis and do-nothingness. The precordial pain and numbness vary, but have been present since I first noticed them in May, shortly after I missed the step of a moving street car and found myself flung rather violently on a hard pavement. As to diet. I am a light eater, and weighed last May 175, instead of the 215 when you saw me last. But I shall keep out of the hospital as long as I can. It is tough on Jennie and Carl.

Hope you and yours are all well, and that you enjoyed your leave. Love from us all to all of you, and may God bless and keep you. Am typing this as my writing is not so good. Handwriting aside, the most economical and effective method of obtaining correct data in this matter is for you to visit Copenhagen formally. Genealogical sharks are unreliable and milk you many times over what a trip would cost you.

There is a letter somewhere around here dated 1781, an heirloom, written by his wife to Fr. Smeedorf Birch, our great poet ancestor, who was the friend and contemporary of Fr. von Schiller, and acquaintance of Thomas Gray, author of the "Elegy in a Country Churchyard."

N.

The next summer, Major and Mrs. Anderson visited West Point, likely his first visit back since his 1914 graduation.

September 3, 1931

Dearest mother:

We have fallen in love with West Point all over again. We have wished so many times that you and Tudy were with us. We ought to plan another visit to include us all next time.

Love, Andy

After service with the War Department came service with the Thirteenth Field Artillery Brigade in Fort Bragg, North Carolina.

WAR DEPARTMENT
WAR DEPARTMENT GENERAL STAFF
PERSONNEL DIVISION G-1
WASHINGTON

July 1, 1932.

Major John B. Anderson, G.S.C.,
Washington, D.C.

My dear Major Anderson:

Your detail on the War Department General Staff has expired by law.

On the occasion of your relief from duty in this office and departure for your new station, I wish to express my sincere appreciation of the excellence of your work and its value to the Army. In your capacity as Executive Officer of the Personnel Division the relationship between us has been very close and at all times both pleasant and satisfactory. Your sound judgment and careful thought have been of great assistance to me personally as well as to the work of the Personnel Division.

I wish you all success in your new assignment.

Sincerely,

ANDREW MOSES,
Brigadier General,
Assistant Chief of Staff.

**Commendation Letter from Brigadier
General Andrew Moses, 1932**

Part of his service at Fort Bragg included an assignment with the Civilian Conservation Corps (CCC), a New Deal program enacted by the Roosevelt administration to cope with high unemployment during the Great Depression. This assignment gave him experience in the organization and motivation of civilians for quasimilitary service, an experience that proved valuable in the rapid Army expansion of 1939-1942. CCC jobs were given to many of the Bonus Army, out-of-work veterans of World War I.

In 1934, Major and Mrs. Anderson, with daughter Tudy in tow, returned to the Command and General Staff School at Fort Leavenworth. The Great Depression was a quiet time for the Army. For Major Anderson, it afforded time to spend with family and friends. The strength of his faith deepened here with regular visits to the Memorial Chapel at Fort Leavenworth.

Home Anniversary Card

Unlike 1924, when he arrived as a student, this time he joined the faculty of the Command and General Staff School for a four-year tour of duty as an instructor. Fellow faculty members from 1934-1938 included Edward Brooks, Manton Eddy, Wade Haislip, Frank

Milburn, and Lucian Truscott. Anderson and his colleagues not only had the opportunity to teach, they had the opportunity to get to know each other well.

On a professional level, it was a time of heated debate about the proper structure of the Army, particularly the size and structure of the infantry. Some infantry officers believed that the larger four-regiment division, which provided mutual support during defensive operations, was best suited for combat. They believed that the next war would resemble the First World War and that the lessons of that war were best applied to current military doctrine. Others, like Lesley McNair and Bradley Chynoweth, argued for a three-regiment division that was more suitable for offensive operations, more adaptable to changing conditions in the field, and more likely to exploit enemy weaknesses. The doctrine of mobile warfare with motorized infantry units and individual tank units capable of independent exploitation of opportunities in the field prevailed. The discussions "gored" some of the sacred cows of the Army, including, but not limited to, the removal of horses and mules from active service. Command and General Staff School instructors would mold the next generations of combat commanders.

On a personal level, social obligations were part of life at Fort Leavenworth. West Point alumni reveled in the good fortunes of the Army football team, including a convincing win over Navy: 28-6. One luncheon program included the lyrics of the "West Point Alma Mater," Army football cheers, and humorous songs of the day. The songs and cheers stoked the fires of the West Point spirit, especially for those who had played Army football or had supported the team like Major Anderson, the "curator" of the Army Mule.

Singing and reminiscing bound the West Point men together; in the near future, they would need each other in many ways. They were well aware of the storm clouds on the horizon. The re-arming of the German Army, the rise of militarism in Japan, and the growing power of Adolf Hitler were viewed as signs that war was coming.

In 1935, after seventeen years as a major, and seventeen years after his temporary appointment as a lieutenant colonel, Anderson attained the permanent rank of lieutenant colonel. More promotions seemed likely.

In 1937, he received this letter from Nels:

February 28, 1937   San Francisco, California

Dear Brother:

Some years ago, you asked me for some information regarding some of our ancestry. Although at the time I answered you discouragingly, and I still have the Westerner's outlook, that a man is what he is, whether his forebears go back to a horse thief or a robber baron, I nevertheless wrote to Ruth Bryan Owen, our then minister to Denmark, to please put me in communication with our lady-in-waiting aunt, if so be she yet lived, giving Mrs. Owens what information I had, but which did not include the married name of our aunt, which I could not recall, nor can I now. I never received a reply.

Had I obtained your aunt's address it was my idea to get from her by correspondence some history of our grandfather, legislator and Privy Council to Christian IX, and one of the active founders, I believe, of the present great Danish cooperative. Also of his wife's brother Finsen, governor of Iceland, and father of Dr. Niels Finsen, discoverer of that boon to lupus (skin tuberculosis) sufferers, the Violet Ray. Northern Europe used to be dotted with Finsen hospitals. And going back further, to the poet in our family who is said to have been a friend of T. Gray, of Elegy of Country Churchyard fame, through Schiller or other German poet (Goethe? Heine?) Contemporary with Gray.

I remember mother getting a reply to a letter in which she had sent to our aunt a photograph of yours truly in his first shave-tail uniform taken in Portland, Ore., in 1900, when I was en route to Alaska. That was the last letter that I know of that any of us ever received from her. Thirty-seven years ago. The saying is not always true, but the law of averages makes it mostly so, that we are ever prouder of our ancestors than they would be of us, were they to come back here and look in on us.

I am looking at Army orders in our daily paper these days, expecting, on account of the increase, to see Colonel instead of Lt Col J.B.A. Carl [13] and Bessie are in San Antonio, as you already know, I guess. Getting along fine. Jennie is well. We both send our love to you and Sue and Tudy, a big girl now, I imagine.

San Francisco is about the same, notwithstanding two bridges and an exposition in the offing. The maritime strike is over (not a sit-down

one, by the way) and you can't notice any difference, either. Or am
I getting cynical? God bless and keep you and yours, and write more
often, your loving brother, Nels

The two letters from Nels, his photograph in uniform from the
Spanish-American War, and his book of poetry paint a picture of
this loving man, this older brother who advised his sibling to join the
Army, who devoted himself to his family and church, and who was
to die in 1942 without seeing his younger brother again. His quiet
devotion to family and God, and his insights into human affairs,
undoubtedly influenced his brother "Ben."

As world events accelerated, Lieutenant Colonel Anderson
reflected often on his brother's kind yet powerful words. Nels'
statement that "we are ever prouder of our ancestors than they would
be of us, were they to come back here and look in on us" motivated
his younger brother to continue to strive for excellence.

Lieutenant Colonel Anderson's career was on the rise and
prospects for promotion were increasing as the United States
military came to the realization that war in Europe was inevitable.
The Anschluss[14] of Austria into the Third Reich occurred in March
of 1938 and set the stage for further German expansion. The Munich
Agreement of September 1938 accepting the German demand for the
immediate occupation of the Sudetenland was authored by Hermann
Goering, proposed by Benito Mussolini, and agreed to by French
Prime Minister Edouard Daladier and British Prime Minister Neville
Chamberlin. In uttering the famous phrase "Peace in our time,"
Chamberlin believed the Allies had arrived at a political solution
to Germany's expansionary demands. Others saw the Munich
Agreement as evidence of the Allies' lack of political will and an act
of appeasement. In accordance with the terms of the agreement,
the Sudetenland was occupied in October 1938. Shortly thereafter,
in March 1939, Germany invaded the remainder of Czechoslovakia.
The world stage was set for war.

In June 1939, Anderson attended his West Point Class of 1914
twenty-fifth reunion. Although some class members had died in
World War I, training accidents, or other conflicts around the world,
most of them remained on active duty and were in positions of ever-
increasing responsibility.

West Point Class of 1914 25th Class Reunion Photograph, 1939
Anderson is standing in the front rank second from the right.

The members of the West Point Class of 1939 were undoubtedly following world events with great interest. Many officers were already stationed in Washington, DC, preparing themselves and the nation for war.

With the invasion of Poland on September 1, 1939, World War II in Europe began. The Army accelerated its plans for what it viewed as a likely resumption of hostilities around the globe. While giving the military some leeway in its preparations, President Franklin D. Roosevelt's administration was treading very carefully. Isolationism was a strong political force in the United States in the 1930s. Many Americans were convinced that the US was foolish to have ever become involved in World War I. They felt that the human and financial costs of the war outweighed any benefits we had received. In addition, large ethnic groups in the United States opposed any support of the British and their empire. Irish, Italian, and German immigrants opposed any United States intervention in European affairs, especially on the side of the British or French. The US ambassador to England, Joseph P. Kennedy, an Irishman by heritage and the father of the future president John F. Kennedy, actively preached appeasement and sought an accommodation with Hitler and the Third Reich.

After the British and French defeat at the Battle of Dunkirk in early June 1940, an attitude shift began. Americans began to realize the German threat to Western democracy. The words of Winston Churchill began to make more sense. When France surrendered to Germany on June 22, 1940, Germany divided the country in two and occupied northern France. From northern France, the Germans planned to invade England. Field Marshal Petain, the hero of France in World War I, collaborated with the Germans, was named leader of the Vichy government, and governed the southern half of France. Over the summer of 1940, England staved off invasion by the German Army in large part by the heroic efforts of the Royal Air Force.

The United States still kept up the pretense of neutrality. An act of Congress, the 1940 Destroyers for Bases Agreement, gave England fifty obsolete US Navy destroyers in exchange for US access to ports in the Caribbean, Bermuda, and Newfoundland. The United States was selling war materials to England for gold, a requirement of the US Neutrality Acts of the 1930s.

By early 1941, England was bankrupt. It had no more gold or money to pay for war materials. Hampered by an ambivalent public and the constraints of the Neutrality Acts, President Roosevelt came up with the idea of "Lend Lease." The "Lend Lease" policy was explained to the American people as an aid program: "Would one not lend a hose to a neighbor whose home was on fire? If the hose were damaged, a good neighbor would withhold any payment demands until the crisis had passed." With that homey explanation, the Roosevelt administration used the "Lend Lease" program to distribute food, oil, and material to England. It effectively ended the pretense of neutrality.

While political events moved the country ever closer to open conflict with Germany and Japan, Washington society continued as before. The Andersons joined many Washington notables, like Mary Frances Rollow, Margaret Eisinger, and Melville Grosvenor, in evenings of ice skating, dancing, and fantasy. These events had the air of Nero fiddling while Rome burned.

As Washington high society ice skated, Europe was ablaze. Yugoslavia was under attack by the Germans; Field Marshal Ervin Rommel, the famed "Desert Fox," attacked Tobruk in North Africa; heavy convoy losses by German U-boats were mounting in the

Atlantic; and the German battleship *Bismarck* entered the North Atlantic, sank *HMS Hood*, and was itself destroyed in the Bay of Biscay by a combined air and surface force of the Royal Navy.

In June 1941, Hitler attacked the Soviet Union. Hitler's Operation Barbarossa ended the uneasy peace of the Molotov-Ribbentrop Pact. The German three-pronged attack toward Moscow, Leningrad, and the southern oil fields of the Caucasus rolled back the Russian forces. The attack was spectacularly successful. There was little indication that anything could stop the Germans, either in Europe or Russia. The British and the Russians were desperate to preserve good relations with the Americans and the vital war material America provided.

As the ripples of war continued, the US Army expanded and promotions came faster. In June 1941, just six years after his last promotion, Lieutenant Colonel Anderson was once again moved up the ranks, this time to colonel. But then, from a peacetime low of less than 150,000 men to an army greater than a million men, the Army suddenly needed more generals. And so, just four months after his promotion to colonel, Brigadier General Anderson was introduced to the world.

The Russians courted anyone who might aid them in their fight against Germany. Brigadier General and Mrs. Anderson were invited to attend the celebration of the twenty-fourth anniversary of the Great October Socialist Revolution. This invitation of the Charge d'Affaires and Mrs. Gromyko of the Union of Soviet Socialist Republics on November 7, 1941, was their last official social obligation in Washington.

Brigadier General Anderson left Washington less than two weeks later to assume command of the Artillery of the Second Infantry Division stationed at Fort Sam Houston, San Antonio, Texas. He joined the division's commanding general, Brigadier General John C. H. Lee, a military engineer by training and member of the West Point Class of 1909. The Second Infantry Division was known as "The Indian Head" Division by virtue of its distinguished shoulder patch.

Brigadier General Anderson in Sam Browne Belt, July 1942

For Brigadier General Anderson, this assignment was an exhilarating moment in his career. Only two years before, Lieutenant Colonel Anderson had attended his twenty-fifth West Point class reunion. His duty station at the time was a desk job in Washington, DC, at the War Department. Despite all his training, his experience in France in World War I, and his excellence as a student at the Command and General Staff College, he feared world events would pass him by. Now, with war close on the horizon, he was assigned to an active combat unit for duty in his area of expertise: field artillery. He was returning to Texas, where his active military career had begun in the summer of 1914.

CHAPTER 6

SECOND INFANTRY DIVISION ARTILLERY COMMANDER AND COMMANDING GENERAL 102ND INFANTRY DIVISION

1941-1943

The US Army was expanding rapidly. From a third-rate military power in 1939, the Army had increased its strength ninefold to more than 1,650,000 officers and men by early 1942. This expansion placed a great responsibility on the shoulders of regular Army officers like Brigadier General Anderson.

The Second Infantry Division was the first US Army division to be reorganized as a triangular division, the brainchild of General Anderson's mentor Lieutenant General Lesley McNair. With advances in tank technology and mechanized infantry units, the doctrine of static trench warfare was now obsolete. As seen in the German Army's use of blitzkrieg tactics in Poland, France, and Russia, combined air and ground operations of highly mechanized tank and mobile infantry units were best able to exploit an enemy's weaknesses. The old, ponderous four-regiment rectangular division was abandoned for a more mobile three-regiment triangular division.

In 1941 and 1942, changes in field artillery doctrine complemented the changes in division structure. Spotter aircraft coordinated with forward artillery observers. Trucks, jeeps, and half-track vehicles replaced horses and mule-drawn caissons. General Anderson was brought from the Office of Field Artillery of the War Department to the Second Infantry Division to make these changes in the Second Infantry. He brought a wealth of practical knowledge and combat and instructional experience to the task. In short order, he brought the Artillery of the Second Infantry to higher levels of proficiency in modern, mechanized warfare. The reward for progress made was the transfer of trained personnel, or cadres, from the Second Infantry to newly formed artillery units of the Eighty-fifth and 102nd infantry divisions.

On May 16, 1942, Nels died in San Francisco. Brigadier General Anderson's duties prevented him from attending the funeral. At this time of war, there was little time to mourn.

A letter he sent to his wife, Sue, written two weeks after Nels' death, hints at his sadness but quickly reverts to the more practical and mundane matters of the day.

May 31st, 1942
Fort Sam Houston, San Antonio, Texas

Darling:

This is a long day, and I am missing you both. Also, I am wondering if you made your connection in New Orleans, as the train was at least 45 minutes late out of here yesterday. I assume you did make it, however, or I probably would have heard from you.

I am enclosing a telegram for Tudy, which arrived just after I reached home yesterday. I opened it, thinking it might be from Mother, but as soon as I realized it was a congratulatory telegram I stopped reading it. So, tell Tudy I didn't read it, nor do I know from whom it came.

Watkins, of course, lost out on his furlough because of the restrictions placed on leaves and furloughs by the Third Army. He didn't seem to mind, however.

No news to tell you. The party last night was very nice, but I came home about 10:15 and went to bed. Our table was on the terrace, next to the pool, and it was delightfully cool and pleasant. However, I didn't enjoy it as I was lonesome for you.

Write me if you find the time. Love to mother, Tudy and to yourself, darling. All my love and kisses to you.

As ever, Always yours, Andy

Shortly after Anderson wrote this letter, and in recognition of his work with the Second Infantry, he was detached from the Second Infantry and named commanding general of the new 102nd Infantry Division, nicknamed the "Ozarks." The initial cadre of officers and men for the 102nd had come from the Second Infantry, making his assignment a logical one. With it, Anderson and his family moved again, this time from Fort Sam Houston, San Antonio, to the newly constructed Camp Maxey in Paris, Texas, on the Texas-Oklahoma border.

Major General Anderson Receives His Second Star, 1942

In the summer of 1942, Brigadier General Anderson was promoted to major general. Professional and family concerns kept him busy. His wife and daughter left Camp Maxey abruptly to attend to the health of Judge George Palmer, who suffered a heart attack that summer, an illness from which he would not recover. For Anderson, the loss of his brother in May and the serious illness of his father-in-law, a man beloved for his generosity, sense of humor, teasing nature, and decency, must have seemed a cruel turn of events. At the time of his greatest achievements, many whom he admired and with whom he would have enjoyed sharing them were dead, ill, or absent.

August 25th, 1942
Camp Maxey, Texas

Darling:

Just a note to tell you I miss you and Tudy and to express the hope Daddy will be better upon your arrival, and that he will soon be entirely recovered.

Am enclosing mother's letter which arrived this evening and Bobby C.'s telegram. I didn't know what to do about Bobby, but am assuming that Tudy has wired him about her departure.

"Big Mac" [15] just came by and I took him around to the Switzer's, after explaining your and Tudy's sudden departure. He expressed his sympathy and the hope you would find daddy better upon your arrival.

Clara says to return the sugar ration cards, or, if you left them here, to let us know where they are.

After the interruption by "Big Mac" I didn't look back to see if I had mentioned this.

Sent a wire to mother tonight telling of your arrival. Give mother and daddy my love, and tell Daddy he may be down, but I know he is not out, and that he'll be up and going strong again soon.

Write me, darling, and I'll try to drop at least a line in the mail box each day.

All my love to all of you. My best love and kisses to you, precious. As ever, Always yours, Andy

There was little time for sadness or reflection. During the summer of 1942, increasing numbers of enlisted men and officers arrived at Camp Maxey. Soon, the officer ranks swelled to more than 100.

August 29th, 1942
Camp Maxey, Paris, Texas

Darling:

Received your telegram yesterday and was so glad to hear that daddy was better and that you had withstood the trip and had arrived safely. Had hoped I'd have a letter from you today, but I know you are worn out and that it is always difficult to get down to letter writing immediately after your arrival.

Had a nice dinner and evening with the Switzers last night and they, too, were delighted to hear the news in your telegram. Ruthie left yesterday morning, with Mary Keyser,[16] for Fort Sill, but I suppose Ruthie will be back in a day or so as she begins working at the exchange on Tuesday.

Went by and got Donnie on the way home from camp this afternoon. He looks well, though thin. His nose is cool, he is very active, and yelps the minute I leave him alone. The mange seems to have almost disappeared, or is healed at any rate, although he still scratches quite a lot. The total bill was $5.00, which certainly could not be called anything but very reasonable. Wish I could find a few more like Dr. Cook here in Paris in the matter of charges, at least.

After our hot Thursday, it turned cool in the night and has been delightful ever since. My only complaint is I am missing you and Tudy. It is always doubly lonesome on Saturdays and Sundays.

All seems to be going along alright at camp. The days are slipping by and I can't realize that we'll begin to fill up about two weeks from now. Hope you'll be back before then.

I sincerely hope daddy is better and that he will continue to improve rapidly. Give mother and daddy both my love.

Write me, darling, and tell me all about yourself, your trip, and when you expect you may be able to return. All my love and kisses to you, precious, and to Tudy.

As ever, Always yours, Andy

September 2, 1942

   Darling:

   Received your wire yesterday and was so sorry daddy was not feeling so well. And, of course, I was selfish enough to be disappointed that your return home had to be postponed. I do hope daddy will be better soon, and that he will continue to improve until he fully regains his health. If you feel you should remain, don't hesitate to do so, for, although I miss you and Tudy terribly, I'm getting along alright.

   Had a letter from Mr. Fleming[17] yesterday with the expected answer from the old devil McDonald. I replied to it today saying I was making every possible legal effort to break the lease, and I think I can do it. Major Perell is looking into the matter for me. Fleming as much as told me not to bother him further with the matter as he was not McDonald's agent in the case. I politely told him that since McDonald had not indicated his agent nor given me his (McDonald's) address, I was forced to deal with the latter through the agency to which I paid the rent—in this case, Mr. Fleming's department in the bank. I'll probably be as popular as a skunk in a parlor with all these bohunks here in Paris, before I get away from the dump.

   Went to Hugo and was bored stiff for over an hour listening to a lot of bunk and hooey by Senator Thomas.[18] His statements regarding the army, the war effort, in fact everything he said, was inaccurate and misleading to a very large degree. He isn't running for reelection this year, otherwise his speech probably would have been worse. Didn't get to bed until 11:30, which was the worst part of the evening.

   Not much news except Lou Busbee[19] has arrived. She is at the Gibraltar temporarily, but I haven't seen her yet.

   Miss not having any letters from you, but the telegram was better than nothing.

   Come home as soon as you feel you can leave, I miss you so.

   Love to mother, daddy and Tudy, and all my love and kisses to you, precious. As ever, Yours, Andy

   P.S. Mr. Palmer[20] asked me over this evening to
   play dominoes!!!   A.

Sadly, the illness of General Anderson's father-in-law prevented his wife and daughter from attending the 102nd activation ceremony, an event that, to date, represented the pinnacle of General Anderson's career.

The headlines read, "The latest edition to Lieut. Gen. Walter Krueger's Third Army, the 102d Infantry Division, to be activated at this new Army camp September 15."

Anderson spoke to about 100 civilian guests and the hundreds of officers and men forming the division training cadre. "Time is short and every available time-saving facility is important," he stated. Among his guests were Major General Courtney Hodges,[21] commanding general of the X Army Corps, and Brigadier General John H. Hilldring, commanding general of the Eighty-fourth Infantry Division. Also present were Miss Sallie Lee Lightfoot and Sam Bell Maxey Long, granddaughter and great nephew of General Sam Bell Maxey, for whom Camp Maxey was named.

A week after the day of celebration, presentation, speeches, and ceremony, Anderson received news of the death of his father-in-law, Judge George Currell Palmer, on September 24, 1942.

With no time to mourn, Anderson plunged into the work of creating his new infantry division. He took on the task of organizing from scratch over 15,000 men into an efficient, capable fighting unit at a new camp with roughly constructed wood barracks, no history or tradition, and few charms. All eyes, both at camp and from afar in the War Department, were on the new general. Success or failure would determine his future career.

Fifteen thousand civilians were turned into soldiers—soldiers ready to forget their civilian concerns, soldiers ready to receive commands, and soldiers ready to follow one another into combat. The training and indoctrination were designed to mold them into an effective fighting force. Camp Maxey had its own post office, hospital, commissary, and recreational facilities. His assistant division commander, Brigadier General Alonzo Fox,[22] ably assisted him.

Major General Anderson with General Alonzo Fox, 1942

Getting out of the office was more in line with General Anderson's command style. Out in the sun, away from the telephone, doing troop inspections, giving instructions, and offering encouragement agreed with him. He drove his own jeep with its two-star designation, a 102-X, meaning 102nd Infantry Division, and HQ-3, denoting that the jeep was from the headquarters' motor pool. He was hard to miss; the soldiers in the field could see him coming a mile away. That was the idea!

General Anderson in 102nd Headquarters Jeep, Camp Maxey, Texas, 1942.

**Sue 'Tudy' Anderson with Beau,
Washington, DC, Summer, 1943.**

As the weeks and months of training passed, the realism of training increased. In the autumn of 1942, the Army, Navy, and Marine Corps stopped the Japanese march toward Australia with bloody victories in the Battle of Guadalcanal and the Battle of the Coral Sea. In North Africa, Operation Torch began the Americans' direct involvement in the European war. By November 1942, the British, under General Bernard Montgomery, forced Field Marshal Rommel to retreat from El Alamein. War was raging, and the 102nd was preparing to join the fight.

The training intensified with the construction of a "German" town replete with booby traps and pseudo-Nazi flags. At the time, the United States had only just invaded North Africa at Casablanca, Oman, and Algiers. The battle at Kasserine Pass would not occur until February 1943. The invasion of Sicily, Italy, and France were only plans in the minds of staff operations officers and in the drawers of the War Department. And yet the preparations of the 102nd for an invasion of Europe became more realistic and focused. The emphasis on urban combat suggested the future of the division. Days, weeks, and months of hardship and loneliness lay ahead.

In the autumn of 1942, before settling down to Thanksgiving dinner, the officers and enlisted men of the 102nd Infantry Division at Camp Maxey heard General Anderson deliver the following address:

November 26, 1942

> *"Today we, as a nation, are giving thanks for the blessings that have been bestowed upon us during the past year. It is our first Thanksgiving Day since the cowardly attack at Pearl Harbor which plunged us into this war.*
>
> *"Perhaps we feel that, as a nation or as individuals*

we have little to be thankful for on this day. Our losses at sea, our reverses on land, and other setbacks in our war effort, have been serious blows to the nation. Your call to the colors, requiring you to leave the comforts of your home, your jobs, and your families may appear to be good reasons why you should not be filled with a thankful spirit on this day.

"Our forefathers, who selected a day for Thanksgiving, suffered many hardships. They expected personal hardships and suffering. Hard labor was the rule. Danger from hostile Indians or from disease was a daily menace. Those of the original settlers who had survived those difficult days felt they had reason to be thankful. Their lives had been spared. Their food supply appeared to be ample for the coming winter months. They had shelter from the elements, and an abiding faith in their ability, with the aid of their God, to carry on. And so, they gave thanks to Him who had spared them and who had granted them the strength and the opportunity to establish themselves in a new land as a people free from the persecution they had suffered in their former homes across the sea.

"Today, we have far greater reasons for thankfulness than did these forefathers of ours. As we look upon the war-torn way of the world we find whole nations under the heel of a ruthless conqueror— nations that have been bombed and blackened by fire, nations whose able-bodied men not only are facing the dangers of the battlefield and the sea but whose families are in constant danger of death at the hands of a foe who has no scruples in killing or maiming the defenseless women and children of their opponents. We, as a nation, have been spared these calamities. Our homes are intact. We are amply supplied with food and clothing. Our loved ones live in comparatively great safety. And today, our armed forces and those of our Allies are gaining successes against our enemies. Indeed, we have much for which

to give thanks on this Thanksgiving Day.

"As we leave here this morning, let us go with thankful hearts and a full realization of the many blessings that we, as Americans, have been and are enjoying. Let us remember, however, that to retain our privileges and rights as a free people and to remove the tyranny that our enemies have imposed upon the freedom-loving nations of the world, we must be willing to make additional sacrifices and to suffer additional hardships. Let us, in the days to come, follow in the steps of the forefathers who did not flinch in the face of danger or difficulties and who, in the midst of their struggle for freedom and survival, found reasons for a day of thanksgiving.

"Also, as we go our different ways this Thanksgiving Day, let us not only go with thankful hearts but also with hearts filled with a determination that we will each do our full part in the ultimate defeat of the enemies that threaten our freedom and the rights and privileges of all freedom-loving people. Let us dedicate ourselves, without reservation, to this task, in order that a Thanksgiving Day on which we will again find a war-weary world at peace will not be far removed."

General John B. Anderson, CG,
102nd Infantry Division

General Anderson's Thanksgiving Day message emphasized the importance of the men's spiritual needs. Their strength and well-being were to be tested in many ways, and the power of prayer to aid them in their duties was never forgotten. Likewise, Anderson made sure that Easter sunrise services in April 1943 were performed among the blue-bonnet carpeted fields of Texas. As the men prepared for war, these rituals provided spiritual strength and comfort.

Anderson's daughter, Tudy, spent the academic year 1942-1943 at Hockaday School in Dallas. After graduation from the school in June 1943, she enrolled in Mary Baldwin College in Staunton, Virginia, for the academic year 1943-1944. Before she would be off to college, Anderson, like all fathers, hoped to spend some time with his daughter. Understandably lonely for home life like the family had had at Fort Leavenworth from 1935-1939, he hoped that maybe the rapid expansion of the 102nd with thousands of healthy young men at Camp Maxey would entice Tudy to stay awhile in Texas. Unfortunately for him, Tudy had other ideas. While living in Texas, she had maintained ties with friends in Washington, DC. Since she was heading back East for college, she was more interested in reclaiming her life there that had been interrupted by the start of the war.

14 May 1943

Dearest Tudy,

Enclosed is your monthly allowance check, which has been reduced by $10.00 to cover part of the Frost Bros. bill. Hope you are not so filthy rich that you cannot use it.

Mother's and my present plans are to come to Dallas in the car on Saturday afternoon, May 29th. Will you call the Baker and reserve a double room for us for the night of the 29th, and ask them to notify me if a reservation will be available?

We are looking forward to seeing you and bringing you home with us. We (the Division) are making a lot of plans for well-known orchestras, broadcasts, etc., for Maxey during June. So, you'd better not plan on running away from us too fast. You might miss a lot, including the 3500 college boys who are beginning to arrive in Col. Sands' stockade.

Love from mother and me. Will see you soon.

As ever, Your daddy

All during the long, hot summer of 1943, the cannons banged away at Camp Maxey. The training of the field artillery was a top priority of General Anderson. From his experience in France in World War I, he knew that field artillery was more than just banging away with cannon fire. Counterfire by the enemy was deadly and accurate. The need for deep gun emplacements requires hard manual labor to dig the gun pits and position the guns properly. Likewise, the ammo-carrying jeeps and shell depots needed protection or all would be lost. Last, also a lesson from the field in World War I, camouflage was an essential element to the survival of the guns and men of the field artillery.

Anderson often carried a "swagger stick" with him in the field, a tradition of the British Army that no doubt impressed him during his duty with that army in Ypres in February and March of 1918. His quiet appreciation of the traditions of the British Army was reflected in many aspects of his leadership. He gave credit where credit was due. He gave encouragement to his officers and men. He was seen in the field as often as possible. He was one who understood well the tradition of Winston Churchill to be seen at the front with his men. Undoubtedly, he knew the troops enjoyed seeing their general out and about, not pent up in headquarters.

By the summer of 1943, the 102nd Division had men from each of the forty-eight states and the District of Columbia, as well as men born in fifty-four foreign countries, including Germany, Italy, and France. Chinese, Filipinos, Poles, and Turks were all part of one military unit dedicated to victory and the elimination of the German Nazi and Japanese regimes. The 102nd Division personnel were topped in strength by Pennsylvania's 1,758 natives. Second were New Jersey's 1,269 men, while Texas was third with 1,216 men.

Everyone was increasingly on edge at the end of that summer. North Africa had been cleared of German and Italian forces in June, and the air campaign against the European continent was intensifying with raids on the oil refineries at Ploesti. The Italian islands of Pantelleria and Lampedusa surrendered to the Allies. Then in July, Operation Husky, the invasion of Sicily, began. Although United States forces were given only a supporting role in the invasion, George Patton, Omar Bradley, and Lucius Truscott were beginning to be noticed for their exploits. The invasion of the mainland of Italy was next. The men of the 102nd knew that the invasion of the mainland of Europe loomed in the near future.

But first, General Anderson and his 102nd Infantry Division needed to pass muster in the 1943 Louisiana Maneuvers, the final examination of readiness of Anderson's 102nd for combat. The exercises gave General George Marshall and his referees an opportunity to evaluate the division's senior leadership. Positive evaluations were considered essential for command of troops in the field.

Major General Anderson in the Field Summer, 1943

Marshall's judgments were considered severe, but fair. The best way to evaluate an older officer was to put them under the stress of combat conditions. From his experience in World War I, Marshall knew mental errors or physical disability of commanding officers resulted in serious problems. He felt every effort was needed to ensure the capabilities of senior leadership. Marshall held to Army policy that officers maintain a high level of physical fitness and that no commander in the command of troops in the field be older than fifty-five. In the first set of maneuvers conducted in Louisiana and the Carolinas in October and November of 1941, only eleven of the forty-two senior commanders who participated were felt capable of command in the field.

General Anderson was put to the task of mental and physical stress both day and night. A photograph of him at the command post of the 406th Infantry Regiment during the 1943 Louisiana Maneuvers shows sweat and deep stress lines on his face. At that time, he was fifty-two years old.

Major General Anderson at Command Post 406 Infantry Regiment, 1943

The widespread and nearly constant use of cigarettes by him and others was one method to cope with the long hours, discomfort, and psychological tension. Whereas other officers rode horses or fished for an escape from the daily grind, Anderson enjoyed few hobbies. Throughout his career, he did enjoy a drink. When Major Chynoweth[23] recalled his time at Fort Leavenworth in 1927, he spoke of enjoying cocktails on Friday evenings with Major

"Swede" Anderson. In later years, Anderson's headquarters went to great lengths to procure the necessary bottles of alcohol for parties, celebrations, and other notable events. The alcohol furthered good feelings and boosted morale. He enjoyed the good fellowship fostered by a cocktail or two.

The 102nd did well in the 1943 Louisiana Maneuvers. They were part of the winning team. Once the maneuvers were concluded, they relaxed a bit, reviewed their performance, and recounted the hardships endured. The experience and criticisms bonded the officers and men.

Cartoons help ease the pain, 1943

Magooke cover 102nd ID
Magazine, 1943

Anderson's success in the Louisiana Maneuvers had an unforeseen consequence. His reward for a job well done with the 102nd was another promotion, this time to command of the newly activated US Army XVI Corps. The promotion must have been bittersweet. He had lived and trained with the men of the 102nd for nearly eighteen months. He had nurtured the unit from nothing than more than a piece of paper to an increasingly capable combat unit. He had fully expected to lead these men in combat, but it was not to be.

He turned the division over to its artillery commander, Brigadier General Charles M. Busbee, and bade farewell during a formal division review parade.

Major General John B. Anderson
DIVISION REVIEW, 29 DECEMBER, 1943

Major General Anderson Farewell Address, December 1943

The 1944 edition of the *Magazine of the 102nd Infantry Division* recounts the event:

> "*The new year brought one disappointment to the men of this division: Major General John B. Anderson, original Commanding Officer of the 102nd, was suddenly transferred to Fort Riley, Kansas, as head of the XVI Corps.*
>
> *"It was with deep and sincere regret that we witnessed his departure, for General Anderson stood for the ideals and the goal to which our training has directed us. The 102nd has been a division for a year and a half. During that time, General Anderson represented us and we, in turn, represented his*

accomplishments as a capable leader. Under his supervision, we changed from the rookies of 1942 to the well-trained division of 1944. To accomplish that was as difficult for General Anderson as it was for us, but his expert guidance led us through the critical period from basic training and maneuvers to the point where every man in the division can look proudly upon himself and realize that his past performance in teamwork has given him a new value; readiness for combat duty.

"General Anderson's presence was known to and welcomed by the entire division. He was a familiar figure on the rifle ranges and elsewhere over the training areas. He would arrive unexpectedly, driving his jeep, and each soldier who was struggling to master the intricacies of battle received encouragement from the friendly smile he had for everyone.

"The Division Review, originally scheduled for New Year's Day, was hastily moved up to December 29th, in honor of General Anderson, when his departure was announced. In his farewell to us on that day, he told us he had seen the 102nd grow from a 'mere scrap of paper' to a division of which he would always be proud, and that he would continue to think of himself as a part of it. And we shall continue to think of him as one of us. His transfer was a shock to the division; not to our training, nor to our morale. It was something more personal than that, for it meant the loss of a friend and leader, a fine officer and a great gentleman.

"The personnel of this division would like to return the compliment given us by General Anderson in his speech of farewell. His closing words were his blessing to us and now, to our former Commander, we say:

"GOODBYE, SIR, AND MAY GOD
BLESS YOU, TOO!"

Anderson received his orders to the new XVI Corps. Like the task of creating the 102nd Infantry Division, the XVI Corps existed initially only as a piece of paper. The XVI Corps would receive officers from almost all sections of the United States and a cadre of enlisted men from Headquarters III Corps. Its traditions, policies, and procedures would soon begin development under Anderson's guidance and direction.

On January 4, 1944, Anderson arrived in Fort Riley and assumed command of the XVI Corps of the Army.

CHAPTER 7

THE XVI CORPS PREPARES FOR WAR

1944

T he activation of the XVI Corps on December 7, 1943, added another corps to the expanding US Army. On December 28, 1943, Anderson received orders to command the XVI Corps at Fort Riley, Kansas. First units were assigned on January 1, 1944. Owing to the unique design of its shoulder patch created by Technical Sergeant Howard M. Sargeant of the Corps Artillery Headquarters, the corps soon became known as the Compass Corps. Command of the XVI Corps was to represent the pinnacle of Major General Anderson's military career.

XVI Corps Patch, The Compass Corps

Corps command is a position of significant authority and responsibility. A corps is the unit designated by the US Army as "the key headquarters for employing all combat elements in proper tactical combinations." A corps commander is responsible for the direction and management of two or three infantry divisions numbering 12,000 men apiece, each division commanded by a major general who is assisted by two or three brigadier generals, one of whom would command the divisional artillery unit. Each division has three infantry regiments, each commanded by a colonel.

Typically, the corps commander is also assigned an armored division consisting of a major general, two or three brigadier generals, and about 400 tanks. In addition, the corps commander has his own artillery resources. All told, this commander is responsible for about 50,000 men. Depending on the task at hand, a corps is augmented with additional specialized engineering, signal, medical and civil administration units. To manage these assets, the corps commander has a chief of staff, an artillery commander, quartermaster, surgeon, and other officers and men numbering about 4,000 under his direct command.

A corps commander is the highest-level officer in the field directly involved in combat operations. For a professional officer, corps command is the ultimate position of tactical leadership. As Major General Wade H. Haislip[24] stated, "The corps commander is the last man towards the rear who directs tactical fire on the enemy." General Matthew B. Ridgway described the corps commander as the one "responsible for a large sector of a battle area. . . . He must be a man of great flexibility of mind, for he may be fighting six divisions one day and one division the next as higher commanders transfer divisions to and from his corps . . ."[25]

Thirty-four general officers commanded combat corps units in World War II. Many of this group entered active duty before, during, or immediately after World War I. They attended the schools established by the Army for advanced command training and had multiple tours of duty as commanders, teachers, and staff officers. West Point graduates provided the majority of the corps commanders. Major General Charles H. Corlett, one of the thirty-four who commanded combat corps units in World War II, recalled the value of the West Point experience saying, "Aside from the academic and military knowledge acquired, the fixed and unalterable code of conduct became part of us."[26]

In addition to this code of conduct, personal experiences at West Point in the classroom and on the athletic field marked many for future greatness. At West Point, Omar Bradley was described as a great baseball player who "some of us will someday be bragging to

our grandchildren that General Bradley was a classmate of mine."[27]
During his time at West Point, future Army Chief of Staff J. Lawton
Collins' character was described as "first, concentration and decision,
second, rapid and hearty action."[28]

Combat experience in the Mexican Punitive Expedition and
World War I was typical of these West Point graduates. George S.
Patton wounded, and likely killed, three Villistas during his time
with Brigadier General John J. Pershing on the Texas-Mexico
border. Future corps commander Ernest J. Dawley participated in
the Pancho Villa Expedition into Mexico in 1916. Future four-star
General Leonard T. Gerow served in the infantry in the Vera Cruz
phase of the Mexican Campaign.

During World War I, twenty-three of the thirty-four future World
War II corps commanders served in the American Expeditionary
Force. Troy H. Middleton showed calmness under fire; Manton S.
Eddy commanded a machine-gun battalion; Alexander M. Patch led
an infantry battalion; Ernest N. Harmon led a cavalry troop; and
George S. Patton led tanks in combat.

After World War I, these future corps commanders prepared
for the next great conflict. The interwar years were a time of further
training and education at Army schools like the Infantry School at
Fort Benning and the Field Artillery School at Fort Sill.

The final rung on the ladder to command was the Command
and General Staff College at Fort Leavenworth. Thirty-three of the
thirty-four corps commanders in World War II attended this college;
fourteen of the thirty-four were not only graduates but also served
as faculty members—instructors of future corps commanders. Troy
Middleton was a student in 1924 and went on to instruct seventeen
of the thirty-four World War II corps commanders from 1924 to
1928, including General Anderson. Anderson was not only a student
of General Middleton in 1925, he also instructed notables like Matt
Ridgway in 1935 and Lucian Truscott in 1936. This experience on both
sides of the lectern for so many of this group gave them an immediate
and intuitive understanding of common staff procedures and doctrine
essential to the efficient operation of an Army corps unit.

General Anderson's experiences at the college prepared him well
for the task of creating the United States Army XVI Corps. While his
peer group included many celebrated Army leaders, his task now was

to create an effective fighting unit. He began with inspection tours across the far-flung units assigned to him. Troops under XVI Corps command were initially scattered over six states, at Camps Carson and Hale in Colorado; Camp Chaffee in Arkansas; Camp Crowder in Missouri; Camp Gruber in Oklahoma; Camps Phillips and Fort Riley in Kansas; and Camp McCoy in Wisconsin. Among the people he visited at Camp Carson in Colorado was his one-time fellow faculty member at the Command and Staff College, Major General Edward Brooks[29] of the Eleventh Armored Division. At Camp Gruber in Muskogee, Oklahoma, he was hosted by Major General J. Lawton Collins, a 1933 graduate of the Command and General Staff College, later Commanding General of the VII Corps, and future Army Chief of Staff.

Major General J. Lawton Collins Welcomes General Anderson, Camp Gruber, Muskogee, Oklahoma, January, 1944.

After this inspection tour, and while awaiting the consolidation of personnel assigned to the XVI Corps headquarters at Fort Riley, Anderson attended an Army Air Corps course to learn the capabilities of current air assets. General Alvan C. Gillem,[30] future commanding general of the XIII Corps, attended the same course. Anderson and Gillem were destined to serve together in General Simpson's Ninth Army.

Anderson's staff was augmented by the arrival of the Corps Artillery commanding general, Brigadier General Charles C. Brown.

Brown was born in Houston, Texas, educated at the Virginia Military Institute, and served overseas in WWI with the Ninety-second Division.

Anderson's chief of staff was Colonel George Barker,[31] who remained with Anderson for the duration of the war and received the Distinguished Service Medal from Anderson in December 1945, for his outstanding wartime service.

The majority of the enlisted men of the headquarters of the XVI Corps were obtained through a cadre transferred from Headquarters III Corps. The XVI Corps Surgeon was Lieutenant Colonel Harold A. Furlong.[32]

Anderson traveled to Watersmeet, Michigan,[33] in March 1944, to observe winter maneuvers of the Seventy-sixth Infantry Division. While there, he conferred with his old friend and mentor Lieutenant General Lesley J. McNair, the commander of Army Ground Forces. General McNair was chief of staff for Army General Headquarters and worked closely with Army Chief of Staff George C. Marshall in the training and evaluation of senior Army officers capable of higher command.

General Anderson Presents Congressional Medal of Honor to Widow of PFC Robert D. Booker, Kearney, Nebraska, January, 1944.

In the spring of 1944, Anderson traveled to Nebraska to perform another important duty: a posthumous presentation of the Congressional Medal of Honor. Receiving the medal was the widow of Private First Class Robert D. Booker, a member of the Thirty-fourth Infantry Division killed in Tunisia on April 9, 1943.

Another duty in the spring of 1944 was of a more political nature. Anderson hosted Undersecretary of War Robert P. Patterson at his headquarters, Fort Riley. Anderson knew that his career required cordial relations with political figures. Apparently, Undersecretary of War Patterson enjoyed Anderson's company well enough in the spring of 1944 to visit his headquarters again in Germany in 1945.

In the meantime, Anderson attended to the many other duties of the commanding general. War bond sales raised money essential for financing the war effort without raising taxes. The United States Treasury issued a huge number of war bonds and received enormous amounts of dollars in sales. Not only did Anderson encourage the public and his men to help finance the war with bond purchases, in his letters home to his family, he encouraged his wife and daughter to buy bonds as gifts and investments in the war effort.

On June 6, 1944, the D-Day invasion occurred. Combined Allied forces landed in Normandy and opened the long-anticipated second front against the Germans. American forces included the First and Twenty-ninth infantry divisions attacking across Omaha Beach (about 21,000 men under V Corps Commanding General Leonard T. Gerow) and the Fourth Infantry Division landing on Utah Beach with the Eighty-second and 101st Airborne divisions parachuted behind German lines (VII Corps under Commanding General J. Lawton Collins).

In July 1944, Anderson's XVI Corps headquarters received a directive from Headquarters Second Army to prepare for movement from overseas on September 1, 1944. They were on their way to join the battle. From the lowest private to the commanding general, excitement was tempered by fear. The reality of war came home to Anderson when he learned that his friend and mentor Lieutenant General McNair was killed on July 25 by short-falling bombs of the US Army Air Force. As part of a plan to break out of the bocage country in Normandy near St. Lo, heavy bombers were used for close air support for infantry operations in Operation Cobra. General McNair had gone forward near the front line when an Eighth Air Force bomb landed in his foxhole. Fortunately, General William H. Simpson, US Ninth Army commander, had declined McNair's invitation to join him at the front to observe the combined air and ground attack.

Anderson and the XVI Corps Headquarters personnel sailed from New York on board the Queen Mary, the majestic Cunard line passenger ship converted to a troop carrier for wartime use. They were joined by Prime Minister Winston Churchill of Great Britain. Churchill was returning from the Second Quebec Conference, where topics had included the Allied occupation zones in defeated

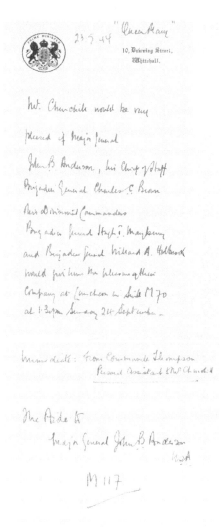

Invitation to lunch with Winston Churchill

Germany, the Morgenthau Plan to demilitarize Germany after the war, and continued Lend-Lease aid to Britain. Churchill's wife, Clementine, attended the conference and was on board the Queen Mary as well.

On the last day of the Atlantic crossing, before dropping anchor in the Firth of Clyde off Greenock Scotland on September 25, Anderson received a note from Commander Thompson, Churchill's personal assistant. The note invited him, his chief of staff, Brigadier General Charles C. Brown, and their divisional commanders, Brigadier General Stephen I. Mayberry and Brigadier General Millard A. Holbrook, to a luncheon in Suite M70. This invitation thrilled Anderson! It was recognition of all the years of sacrifice, loneliness, and family separation. It was vindication for the years of sacrifices of an Army career. He was to dine with the head of the English government, a man whose iron will and gifts of oratory and leadership had led his country and all the English-speaking countries from the brink of defeat to the prospect of victory over Germany.

Both Anderson and Churchill had served in the trenches of Flanders, near Ypres: Churchill in 1916, Anderson in 1918. Did they compare notes or regale each other with stories from the front? Did they discuss different persons from World War I like General John J. Pershing of the American Expeditionary Force or Lieutenant

General Godley, once the commander of II Anzac Corps, and now at age seventy-five the commander of a platoon of the Home Guard? Did the prime minister reaffirm his well-known desire to go forward with the troops, to be at the front whenever possible? Anderson could not have known that he would soon be in a position to indulge Churchill's great desire to be as close to the action as possible.[34]

The XVI Corps headquarters officially opened on September 28, 1944. The XVI Corps was requested by and assigned to Lieutenant General William Hood Simpson's Ninth Army. Simpson was born and raised in Weatherhead, Texas, the son of a Confederate veteran of the Tennessee cavalry. Simpson's father gave him the middle name Hood to honor the great Confederate general from Texas, John Bell Hood. Simpson's father was quoted by his son as being "not too happy to see him in a blue uniform." As Simpson's career unfolded and as his son advanced in the officer ranks, it is said that Simpson's father became resigned to the idea of his son wearing blue and guessed it was "all right."

Although Anderson had no direct ancestors involved in the Civil War, he likely understood well the ambivalence of Civil War veterans and their descendants. He spent years in the Deep South in his training, married a Southern belle, and knew of his father-in-law's sympathy for "The Lost Cause."

Anderson, Class of 1914, and Simpson, Class of 1909, did not know each other at West Point, but their career paths had crossed many times. They had served together on the Texas border during the Mexican War of 1914-1917 and in the American Expeditionary Force in France in World War I. In 1924, Major John B. Anderson was head of the Eighty-third Field Artillery demonstration unit at the Infantry School at Fort Benning while Major William Simpson was a student in the Infantry School. They attended the Army War College together in 1927 in Washington, DC. William "Big Bill" Simpson was tall, completely bald, and widely admired "in the prewar army by officers such as Devers and Harmon for his integrity, earthy sense of humor, intelligence, and kindness." [35] He was married to an English woman, Ruth (Webber) Krakauer, a London-born widow Simpson met while at West Point.

General Simpson, like General Anderson, was an example of a capable officer who spent much of the war stateside training troops for combat. In July 1941, General McNair appointed Simpson first as commanding general of the Thirty-fifth Infantry Division and then as commanding general of the Thirtieth Infantry Division. He did so well that he was given command of the XII Corps in the summer of 1942. His continued record of successful training was so admired that he was promoted to the three-star rank of lieutenant general and given command of the Fourth Army in San Jose, California.

He took the headquarters unit to Fort Sam Houston, where he completed its training before the Fourth Army was renamed and sent overseas as the Third Army. Simpson then received instructions to raise another army headquarters unit, the US Eighth Army. To avoid any confusion with the British Eighth Army in England, Simpson's Eighth Army was redesignated the Ninth Army.

Simpson's command style was widely admired. Even though General Eisenhower had originally proposed another general— General Leonard Gerow, V Corps commander—for command of the Ninth Army, Eisenhower later said of Simpson, "He was the type of leader American soldiers deserve."[36] Eisenhower had thought that General Bradley might "prefer to step up an experienced corps commander ahead of Simpson for command of the fourth U.S. army in the field."[37] Army Chief of Staff Marshall overruled Bradley and Eisenhower. Marshall wished to assure generals like Simpson who trained large formations in the United States that "they would not be excluded from leading them in action overseas."[38]

Even so, command decisions were a source of ongoing backbiting and personality conflicts. As late as October 1, 1944, Eisenhower wrote Marshall, stating, "If I had been able to foresee two or three months ago the actual development in command arrangements, I would probably have advanced a corps commander to take over the Ninth Army." Simpson remained in command, mainly by default because Eisenhower felt that the arrangements had gone so far that it best to follow through.[39]

Like his commanding officer General Simpson, Anderson owed his command position in large part to Army Chief of Staff Marshall's policy of rewarding officers who had trained large numbers of troops in the United States. Anderson also owed his selection as XVI Corps commander in Simpson's Ninth Army to Simpson's specific request that Anderson's XVI Corps be assigned to him. Anderson joined Major

General Alvan Gillem, the commanding officer of the XIII Corps, who in later years made the following statement about Simpson:

> *"We see leadership best reflected, for example, when firmness is substituted for harshness, understanding for intolerance, humanness for bigotry, and when pride replaces egotism. General Simpson's every action exemplified the best of these traits of character. His integrity inspired a high degree of loyalty. His conduct on all occasions was scrupulous, and his associates of all ranks found him to be patient, impartial, courageous, sympathetic, and confident. They also found him equally loyal to seniors and juniors alike. He was an able, respected commander for whom all were willing to give their best endeavors."[40]*

For the first few weeks of Anderson's XVI Corps headquarters unit's service in France in the autumn of 1944, the officers and men served in a logistical and material services function. They facilitated the drivers of the "Red Ball Express"[41] in their efforts to maintain the flow of supplies to the front. The ports of Marseille, Cherbourg, and Brest had fallen to the Allies, but the Germans had wrecked the harbor facilities. The length of the supply line slowed the American and British armies' advance into the low countries and Germany.

In other war news from September 1944, the first V-2 rockets began to fall on London and pressure built up to push the Germans out of the Netherlands and the rocket-launching sites. Operation Market Garden was conceived by Field Marshal Montgomery as a combined Allied effort to eliminate this threat and leap across the Rhine in the northern Netherlands. The supply demands of Operation Market Garden aggravated US Army logistical problems and strained relationships among the generals commanding armies in the field. The focus on this single thrust afforded the Germans an opportunity to regroup and stiffen resistance along the Western Front.

Operation Market Garden, September 17 to 25, failed to reach its objectives and by October, eight V-2 rockets were falling on London daily. Canadian troops entered the lowlands and liberated most of Belgium. Still, the Germans held most of the Netherlands.

The US First Army's meat-grinder battle of the Hürtgen Forest began in earnest and the drive eastward toward Germany slowed. As the Americans and British pushed ever closer to the German border and the populous industrial heartland of the Ruhr Valley with its coal mines and steel factories, resistance stiffened and infantry casualties mounted. For those concerned about the possibility of missing the war, there was plenty of fighting left.

In November 1944, Anderson began a series of letters to his wife, daughter, and his mother-in-law. As a commanding officer, he was rigid in his adherence to censoring requirements. All letters were scrupulously self-censored for information about location, unit, and current activity. Therefore, instead of any real news, gossip about friends and personal items filled the letters, as well as continued pleas for more mail and news from home. However, once news was "released," his letters became a wealth of firsthand information of his experiences.

24 November 1944
Barneville, France

My precious,

Thanksgiving, besides providing us with an enormous turkey dinner, also brought me a letter from you which I enjoyed far more than the dinner. The letter was mailed on the 15th of November, or eight days only to reach me. I have about given up hope of receiving the letters that are missing between October 22nd and November 14th. Also, I am sure earlier dated letters are also missing. Of course, every now and then letters come poking along that have been mailed in September, such as the Gittings' bill, which I sent you a few days ago.

Still can't tell you where I am, except it is one of the places you mentioned in your letter, and farthest south. The weather is terrific and gets worse as winter approaches. It has rained practically continuously for the past three days. Fortunately, when it rains it is not so cold as when it is clear—which rarely occurs.

"Doc" Cook[42] had some blood circulation difficulty. I'm not sure just how it affected him. It may be connected with his earlier trouble, which was thyroid, I believe. The papers have announced that Matt Eddy[43] has his (Doc's) old command, so I suppose you know that.

Our Tudy must be a smart girl, though she never tells us about herself. But we know she has never overdone studying, and yet has made good marks and stood well in her classes. She apparently absorbs matters quickly, and also retains them.

I'll be glad to get the sweater, darling, and thanks for sending it. With all the layers of clothes we wear, 42 will be just right for size. Hope it comes through soon so I can get this sleeveless one washed—I haven't been able to keep it off long enough to have that done.

Your letter certainly helped cheer up an otherwise cheerless Thanksgiving. Hope more will come soon. All my love and kisses, darling, to you and Tudy.

As ever, Always yours, Andy

CHAPTER 8

XVI CORPS:
THE BATTLE OF THE BULGE
1944-1945

In December 1944, the XVI Corps Headquarters moved into Belgium and joined Simpson's Ninth Army at the front. Tongres, Belgium, was the location of the headquarters of the XVI Corps and was on the southern shoulder of the Ninth Army area of responsibility.

Generals Anderson and Simpson with British Major General L.O. Lyne, Commander of the 7th Armored Division, the famed "Desert Rats"

Preparations were underway for the XVI Corps to relieve the British XII Corps in a sector adjacent to the Ninth Army with a planning group going to Beck, Holland, to coordinate the impending operation. As Christmas approached, it seemed like business as usual.

While it was typical business for the Allies, the Germans had other ideas. Hitler had ordered a winter offensive, an attack on the Western Front.

He elected to gamble the fate of Germany on a lightning strike westward. He intended to drive over the Meuse River all the way to Antwerp, destroy all Allied forces north of this thrust, split the Western alliance, and force the Allies to sue for peace. German forces were transferred from the Russian front for the offensive. German Field Marshal von Rundstedt and Field Marshal Model felt the plan unrealistic. They argued with Hitler to scale back the goals of the offensive. Waffen SS General Sepp Dietrich and General der Panzertruppen von Manteuffel joined them in forcefully arguing with Hitler. Their arguments against the overly ambitious military plan were ignored and plans for the offensive continued.

Unknown to the Allies, the Germans amassed supplies and stockpiled ammunition for an all-out attack by 1,400 tanks, 2,000 artillery pieces, and twenty divisions. Even by mid-December, the German intentions remained unknown to the US Army. As Carlo D'Este writes, it "was the latest example of the principle learned and relearned the hard way by the Allies during World War II: Expect the unexpected."[44]

The Germans completed their preparations without arousing the suspicions of the Allies. Instead, the Allies were making plans for Christmas leaves in London and Paris. To relieve tired frontline units, the Americans deployed fresh, untested troops in the Ardennes, an area felt to be a quiet zone and unsuitable for offensive actions by the Germans. The US Army command considered this area appropriate for new and inexperienced units. The Seventy-eighth and 106th infantry divisions, both inexperienced units, were assigned briefly to the XVI Corps during this time, and then moved on.

Because the weather was miserable, cold, and wet, the Americans convinced themselves that the holidays would be a quiet time.

December 4, 1944
Tongres, Belgium

My darling:

What do you think of the homemade Xmas card on the reverse side? It really isn't as bad as far as we are concerned, as the cartoon would indicate. However, it is cold and it is muddy.

Received a Xmas package from Tudy last night which I have dutifully put aside not to be opened until Xmas. I have also refrained from unwrapping any of the contents of your package except the bedroom slippers. I have never received the package you said had been shipped to me from New York. As a matter of record, packages received to date are as follows: one from you, one from Tudy, one from mother, and one from Margaret.[45]

Saw my first cart being drawn by a dog today. I remember as a child in school we were told of the dogs trained to draw carts in Belgium and Holland, but apparently the number so trained now is not very numerous.

The Xmas customs here are quite different from ours. Tomorrow is St. Nicholas day in this vicinity. It is the children's Xmas, whereas the adults' Xmas is on the 25th. The children do not hang up their stockings, but place their wooden shoes by the fireplace along with some hay and carrots or other vegetables. The latter are for St. Nicholas' donkey, which he uses instead of our proverbial reindeer. The church bells have been ringing almost constantly all day today, which I suppose is in anticipation of the celebration tomorrow.

We are having another fairly clear day today, though a few occasional showers have fallen too. But if we get a little sunshine during the day, we don't mind a few showers.

Am well, darling, and hope you and Tudy are too. How are the animals—are their habits improving, or are they as undisciplined and bad as ever?

Write often, precious. All my love and kisses to you and Tudy.

As ever, Always yours, Andy

9 December 1944
Belgium

My darling,

It is snowing heavily this morning—the largest snowflakes I believe I have ever seen. However, the snow is melting as soon as it strikes the ground.

A large consignment of mail came in last evening and everyone received at least two or three letters—except me. I didn't receive a single one, and was I disappointed. Many of the letters were mailed as late as November 27. I can't understand why I didn't receive at least one letter, when the others received so many. George Barker[46] got fifteen. Hope I'll have better luck on the next batch that comes along.[47]

Ever since our arrival over here we have had only powdered eggs for breakfast, and, even though the cooks are quite clever in making them into passable omelets, they are still powdered eggs. But this morning we had real eggs—two of them staring at us on our plates—and it was indeed a real treat. I believe it is the first breakfast I've really enjoyed since I left the States.

We have had our furnace repaired and hope to have it in operation this evening. It is badly rusted out—that is the boiler is—because it has not been in use for about four years, so we do not know whether the repairs made on it will last long or do much good. But if it will stay in operation during our sojourn here it will help some.

We are in a very old town in Belgium, over 2000 years old, and it has quite a history, including occupation by the Romans fifty-odd years before Christ. Tomorrow they are having a special service in the Cathedral—built in the 1200s—for the Americans in this area, during which a brief history of the town will be read in English. I expect to attend, and perhaps will have a better knowledge of my surrounding, from an historical point of view, after such attendance.

While disappointed in not hearing from you last night, I still am hopeful I'll get a batch of letters from you soon. In the meantime, darling, keep on writing as regularly as you can.

All my love, precious, and all my kisses to you and Tudy.

As ever, Always yours, Andy

The cold and snow masked the German's final preparations for their attack in the Ardennes. Anderson's letters are filled with gossip of the comings and goings of officers known to his wife. His hatred of the Germans is also readily apparent.

11 December 1944
Belgium

    Darling,

    I now have heard that Paul was not reduced but sent home for another assignment which may mean a promotion rather than a reduction. I am extremely pleased to know that this is true. And the source of my information for this was Shrimp Milburn who had seen Paul in the U.S. before he (Shrimp) left for over here.

    As you know, or should know, now, from the Stars and Stripes clipping I sent you, the old outfit (102nd Infantry Division, Ozark) is up here in the same army with us. I expect to visit them within a few days. As I have told you before, they are making a splendid reputation for themselves and I am sure they will continue to deliver a fine performance.

    You said in your letter that you can't understand how we men can bear to be near each other when baths are so infrequent. Well, in the first place it is so cold that we don't do much perspiring and in the second place we probably have so many layers of clothing on that all odors are contained inside them and cannot escape. Recently, however, I have been able to get a bath about twice a week, as we have hot showers in the building we are occupying as a headquarters and I have a bathtub in my quarters. Being in a coal mining region, we have been getting a fairly reasonable allowance of coal for heating water and buildings too.

    So, Terry Allen [48] is getting much publicity at home. He is quite a colorful individual and his new division has been doing excellently. They were thrown into the Holland fight for Antwerp—green as grass—and came out with a splendid record of achievement. As you have seen in the papers, they are going to town in the present fight of the First Army. There is no doubt but what Terry is a real fighter and at his best in a fight.

    I wonder who the columnist referred to when he spoke of the officer who was paying a press agent for good notices. I doubt if he was referring to anyone over here for publicity seeking is very much frowned upon by Brad and Ike (Omar Bradley, Twelfth Army Group Commander, and Dwight Eisenhower, Supreme Allied Commander). I know they wouldn't put up with anything of that nature for a moment. I am inclined to believe it is probably someone on the home front, if there is any truth in the accusation.

Through Judge Case, Lt Col Lawrence C. Case, Judge Advocate of the XVI Corps, I met a local Belgium judge last Saturday. The Belgian spoke fairly good English and I had a very interesting conversation with him. We hear a lot at home regarding the treatment of the people of the occupied countries by the Germans, but I know I was inclined to believe that it was probably somewhat exaggerated. (The extent of German barbarism was beyond the imagination of most Americans. The German population of the United States in the 1930s was the largest ethnic group, characterized by hard work and self-reliance. German nationalism was a real element of the group. Most Americans, even those men who had fought in the trenches of World War I, could not comprehend nor admit to the brutality of Nazi policies.) But when you hear of the things the Germans have done, at first hand, you realize we haven't heard the half of it at home. There cannot be, nor has there been, any exaggeration. For example, this judge spent five months in jail and thirteen months in a concentration camp for the following offenses: For refusing to sentence a man to death for killing one of his own pigs, the pig to be used for feeding himself and his family. For this offense (?) the judge was sentenced to nine months in jail. When a son was born to the judge's wife, he named the boy Winston. For this offense (?) he was given another nine months' sentence. These are facts, believe it or not. Can there be any punishment great enough for people like the Germans? I don't believe there can be.

If only I could have more letters from you, the task of finding something to write about would be very much simplified, as you can see from this long letter. So, keep the letters coming, darling.

In the meantime, all my love and kisses to you and Tudy.

As ever,
Always yours, Andy

A letter to his daughter contains the usual dollop of gossip and weather reporting. Meanwhile, the Germans were ready to pounce.

12 December, 1944
Tongres, Belgium

Dearest Tudy:

Your sweet and thoughtful Xmas card, mailed on November 29th, arrived a couple of days ago. I appreciated it so much, although the sentiments expressed therein were probably a little too flattering to be applied to me. Nevertheless, I loved the card—and I must admit the sentiments also.

Went to a demonstration yesterday where I saw many of the old outfit (102nd Infantry Division from Paris, Texas, days), such as Keating (Major General Frank A. Keating, Ridgewood, New Jersey), Busbee (Brigadier General Charles M. Busbee, USMA '15), Damon (Lieutenant Colonel John C. Damon of El Paso, Texas, commanding officer of the 379th Field Artillery Battalion), and Hannigan (Lieutenant Colonel James P. Hannigan, 380th Field Artillery Battalion). Also, Johnny Uncles was present from another unit. I asked Hannigan how Stan (First Lieutenant Stan Mathews of Rockwell Center, New York) was getting on and he said he was doing fine work—one of the best forward observers in the business, as Hannigan expressed it. So, Stan is getting on alright, is well, and hasn't been hurt. Of course, I realize your interest in him is not too keen, but am sure you like to hear about your friends. (First Lieutenant Stanley L. Matthews, Field Artillery, 102nd Infantry Division, was awarded the Bronze Star medal on January 3, 1945 for heroic achievement in Germany; see citation).

Today started off with rain and snow, but by noon the sun was out, and our planes started their usual parade toward Germany. It is now about four o'clock, and they are streaming back home after delivering their messages to the Jerries—and are there plenty of them! We are always happy to be able to say they are on our side—I'd hate to have to take it, if conditions were reversed.

By the time you receive this I suppose you and mother will have completed your trip and visit to New York. Wish I could be with you, but hope you had a grand time, as I am sure you will have. Maybe by another Xmas we can be together again, and what a wonderful celebration that will be—at least for me. And I'll be willing to celebrate all the remainder of my Xmas days in the U.S., too.

Received your Washington postcard only a few days ago—only took about six weeks to reach me. I still enjoyed it, despite its age.

Write me some time—no matter how brief, your letters will be welcome.

Hoping you have a Merry Xmas and nice trip, and with all my love and kisses to you and mother, I am, as ever, Your devoted daddy

The German attack was launched on December 16, 1944. The 106th Infantry Division bore the brunt of it. General Alan Jones commanded the 106th, which had been assigned an area called the Schnee Eifel, a picturesque region of the Ardennes Forest, felt to be a quiet zone. The 106th had relieved the famed Second Infantry Division in the line. At the time, General Jones assessed his situation and wished to adjust his lines. He felt that the disposition of his men east of the Siegfried Line left them little room to maneuver in case of attack. He was denied permission to move back west of the line. He was told that the symbolic value of having "breached" the vaunted line was more important than his tactical considerations. This decision was to haunt the officers of the 106th for years to come. In fact, one officer, Lieutenant Colonel Malin Craig Jr., the artillery commander of the 106th, the son of former Army Chief of Staff Malin Craig, was to write ruefully of the day his division was not given permission to deploy in more defensible positions.[49]

The 106th would suffer severely at the hands of the Germans during the offensive known as the Battle of the Bulge. More than 7,000 men were captured as two infantry regiments and one artillery battalion were overrun. Many captured members of the division would be sent to the slave labor camp Berga. They were not treated as prisoners of war but would spend the remainder of the war as slave labor in ghastly concentration-camp conditions.

The German offensive included three Panzer armies that raced west in a bold effort to cut the Allied line in two. The northern shoulder of the German advance was the Eisenborn Ridge, an elevated position occupied by US Ninth Army forces. While the battle raged, US forces scrambled at first to contain the German offensive. The town of Bastogne was the site of a heroic stand by the men of the 101st Airborne Division; its acting commanding general, General Anthony McAuliffe, responded to the German surrender demand with one word: "Nuts!" The crossroads of Malmedy was the site of a massacre of American soldiers by members of Joachim Peiper's SS Panzer grenadiers.

It was a time of fear and anxiety among American commanders. Criticism leveled at times at the Americans by Field Marshal Montgomery and his colleagues aggravated relations between the American and British allies. Montgomery had long held the notion that he, not General Eisenhower, should command all Allied ground forces. Resentment of the command relationships extended as far back as North Africa, Sicily, and the Normandy invasion. At times, the disputes and jealousies were open wounds that events like the Battle of the Bulge aggravated further.

Montgomery felt that only he had the experience and strategic view to stem the tide of the German advance and that only he could control the battle that threatened to split the Allied armies. He made no secret of his view that Generals Eisenhower, Bradley, and Hodges were too inexperienced, lacked the proper temperament, and were too far removed to control events on the battlefield.

In response to Montgomery's demands and in recognition that a real threat existed that might split the Allied front, Eisenhower detached Simpson's Ninth Army and Hodges' First Army from Bradley's Twelfth Army Group and put them under Montgomery's command. While readers of history know more about the exploits of Patton's Third Army on the southern shoulder of the Bulge and the "rescue" of the 101st Airborne Division from Bastogne, Simpson's Ninth Army and Hodges' First Army held fast on the Eisenborn Ridge and at St. Vith.

Before the end of December 1944, seven combat divisions and support units totaling nearly 135,000 Ninth Army men had taken over the US First Army sector where the Germans had launched their main offensive. These units were provided willingly by the Ninth Army to the First Army in the spirit of unselfish cooperation and teamwork, the hallmark of Simpson's command. Simpson personally phoned Hodges and offered the Thirtieth Infantry Division and the Second Armored Division. It was to a First Army unit, General Matt Ridgway's XVIII Airborne Corps, that Simpson sent his XVI Corps commander, Major General John Anderson.

Simpson considered the rivalries of command subordinate to the overall Allied effort. Rivalries did not cloud his judgment nor hinder his determination to win the fight against the Germans. If Hodges needed a corps commander, and Simpson could spare Anderson's services, Simpson made Anderson's services available.

25 December 1944
Heerlen, Holland

My Darling:

Little would I have believed a year ago, when we were in Austin, that I would be in Holland on this Xmas day.[50]

It really is a beautiful, clear, crisp day, but that cannot remove my lonesomeness for you and Tudy, and the yearning for being home with you. It is perhaps not a very Christmas like spirit, but we are indeed thankful for the beautiful weather of yesterday and today because we are able to pour our air force on the krauts.[51]

I went to church at 9:00 this morning, and Chaplain Kellogg gave a very fine sermon. I started to say a sextet, but there were about ten soldiers in the group, who sang two selections—Silent Night and Babe of Bethlehem—and they were really good. It was evident they had done a lot of practicing for the occasion. The services were in a very large church here, and the place was filled to overflowing with soldiers. Also, there was a scattering of about 30 Dutch civilians in the audience. I suppose every American's thoughts were far away during the service—I know mine were—but the service and the sermon I know boosted my morale, and I am sure it did the same for the others.

As ever, Always yours, Andy

P.S. The enclosed card from Ike arrived last night. Love, Andy

26 December 1944
Holland, XVIII Airborne Corps Headquarters

My darling:

Another clear, crisp day and a good one for our air to get in some more licks on the krauts. If we can have a few more days like the last three, we should be able to do a lot of damage to the attacking Germans.

As I told you in yesterday's letter, I went to church yesterday morning. I meant to mention the fact that it was rather impressive to see all the men present, carrying their rifles, carbines, or other arms, and wearing their steel helmets. It is the first time in my life that I have had to wear a pistol when I went to church. But that is what the Germans have done to this world. Hope we can soon destroy these barbarians so that that state of affairs can be ended forever.

The enclosed Christmas greeting from General Marshall arrived this morning. Am sending it to you as a matter of interest. A very nice note and especially appreciated coming from a man who, in spite of being probably the busiest man in the United States, can take time out to send his greetings to one of his very junior subordinates.

It is now a quarter to four and the sun is about to disappear below the horizon. That will give you some idea of how short our days up here really are.

Always yours, Andy

After his stay with Ridgway and the XVIII Airborne Corps, Anderson returned to XVI Corps headquarters. The frantic efforts to stem the onslaught of the German attack were paying off, and it was time to get back to the business of pushing into Germany.

31 December 1944
Heerlen, Belgium

My darling:

After a very cold 60-mile ride in a jeep, part of the way in a heavy snowstorm, I arrived back at my headquarters in Holland early yesterday evening. Fortunately, we have a heated house and I was soon thawed out and suffered no ill effects. On my way back, I stopped in to see Simp [Lieutenant General William H. Simpson, US Ninth Army Commanding Officer] for an hour's talk on future developments and plans.

Eddie Parker, Frank Carnes, and Joe Nichols remained with me but a very short time and then were shifted suddenly to another place where they were badly needed. That has happened to all my divisions, and, of course, you can readily understand the reason, in view of the recent news from the Western Front. Don't know just what will come to us next, and have no way of knowing.

I have previously written several times that the old outfit [the 102nd Infantry Division was in the XIX Corps of Simpson's Ninth Army] is very near me, so, of course, you know they are not in the south. I know, of course, that Billy Wyche's [USMA '11] division [Seventy-ninth Infantry Division] was in the south. They have made an outstanding record for themselves, and, at last reports are still doing so.

While I was away on this short period of temporary duty I saw several old friends, including Courtney Hodges [Commanding Officer, US First Army]; Bill Kean [Chief of Staff, US First Army, USMA '18]; Matt Ridgway [Commanding Officer, XVIII Airborne Corps, USMA '17]; Jonnie Field, Busbee's brother-in-law; A. C. Stanford, [Brigadier General, Artillery Officer, US Seventy-fifth Infantry Division, USMA'17] whom you don't know, I am sure; and Faye Prickett [Commanding Officer, US Seventy-fifth Infantry Division, USMA '16] also unknown to you, I believe; and many others whom I knew but I don't believe you know. Bill Kean[52] wished to be remembered to you. His family are living in Birmingham. Faye Prickett's outfit was also with me for a few days, but was transferred because of the emergency.[53]

After yesterday's snowstorm, today has turned out to be a beautiful sunshiny day—the first of its kind since Tuesday. These days are always welcome for it gives our air forces an opportunity to get in some good licks on the krauts, as I have told you so many times before. With good weather, we should be able to give the Nazis a good beating in a very decisive manner. I'm sure we'll do it anyway.

Always yours, Andy

January 2, 1945
Heerlen, Netherlands

My darling:

Yesterday a little Dutch boy about 12 years old, who lives near the house we are occupying, made a formal call at about 6 in the evening and presented me with the enclosed greetings. Jane and Josephine are his younger sisters, but apparently were too bashful to take a part in the presentation ceremony.

I thought it a sweet and cute gesture. The little boy was a typical blond little Dutchman, and so clean he practically shone.

Always yours, Andy

January 7, 1945
Heerlen, Holland

My Darling:

I had an experience yesterday that was rather sobering and one which I feel has made me a more tolerant individual. I have a Jewish chaplain attached to my headquarters now. He joined us very recently. He is an extremely high type, intellectual Jew, and we are already quite attached to him. He found in this town a little synagogue which had been wrecked and defiled in general by the Nazis. Through his efforts, he found the leading Jews in the town and they have restored it so it can be used for their services. On yesterday afternoon they held rededication services, which I was asked to attend, and I did attend.

After the usual thanksgiving services of the Jewish faith, several of the prominent Jews spoke. They spoke first in Dutch and then repeated in English. They did not tell of their personal experiences during the German occupation, but referred to it only in a general way. It was so apparent that they had endured suffering and persecution beyond description during the past few years. The sorrow in their eyes and faces cannot be described. The chaplain told me afterwards that they had been hunted down like wild animals, and many of them had had to remain in hiding throughout the period of occupation. He further said that Protestants and Catholics in the community, and I suppose the same is true throughout Holland, helped to protect and hide the Jews, even though it meant imprisonment or worse for them had they been caught assisting them.

I came away from the services with a greater faith in my fellow man—and that excludes Nazis—and also with the determination to be more tolerant in my attitude toward other races and creeds. It was indeed an impressive occasion, and a concrete example of the type of people that make up Germany and the cruelty of those people. Hope we can soon crush them as they have crushed others.

Hope I'll hear from you today, precious. All my love and kisses to you and Tudy, and how I miss you both.

As ever, Always yours, Andy

Dutch people of all faiths held deep affection for the Allied military forces, who liberated the Dutch in the winter and spring of 1945.

In the early years of the war, it seemed the German Reich was unbeatable, unstoppable, and triumphant everywhere. The war news—heard clandestinely on makeshift radios or smuggled receivers—gave evidence of German conquests of Poland, France, North Africa, and vast parts of Russia. From 1939 to the summer of 1944, resistance to the Germans seemed to be futile.

With the invasion of Normandy in June 1944, the idea of the German "superman" was losing credibility and the idea of liberation was gaining credence. Although Operation Market Garden, the combined British-American effort to cross the Rhine in the north, was unsuccessful, the Dutch saw that the Allies were committed to the defeat of the German Army in the west. There was increasing evidence of Allied might, with B-17s by day and Lancaster bombers by night carrying tons of bombs for the destruction of German cities. Once, liberation had only been a hope, a dream. Now, the key to liberation was survival.

For the people of Heerlen, liberation came in November 1944. For others, it did not occur until March 1945.

January 10, 1945

Dearest Tudy,

The past two days brought us a lot of snow, but today the sun is shining brightly again. And sunny days bring droves of our planes over our heads en-route to Germany with their eggs. It is a pleasant sight—when the planes are ours! Also, days like today enable our planes to give their strong assistance to our ground troops in their struggle to drive the Germans back into Germany, and, I hope, soon to their final defeat.

The news about the invasion of Luzon came over the radio today, and it sounds like everything is going fine in that part of the world. Perhaps we can wind up this war before too many more months have passed.

Again, thanks for your lovely Xmas gift. All my love and kisses to you and mother, from Your daddy

From time to time, Hollywood and Broadway actors came to the front to cheer the troops and to remind them that their efforts were not forgotten.

January 26, 1945

Dearest Tudy:

Last evening, I attended a dinner given in honor of Katherine Cornell and her troupe, who are playing "The Barretts of Wimpole Street" for the troops in this area. I sat between Miss Cornell and her leading man, Aherne, and enjoyed talking with them very much. I succeeded in obtaining their autographs for you on my place card, which I am enclosing. The place card had previously been used for another party and another general, but that doesn't affect the autographs, does it? I won't see the play, as front-line troops are being given first priority, as they should be.[54]

Again, dearest, thanks for the sweet Valentine and your thought of me. All my love and kisses to you and mother. As ever, your daddy

War news from Europe and abroad was discussed when possible.

February 5, 1945
Sittard, Holland

My darling:

We are all so pleased that Manila has been recaptured. MacArthur certainly has done a grand job in that campaign. Yes, the initial landing was made along the coast where we stopped that time on our way to or from Baguio, I've forgotten which. Damortis is the name of the place. We who have been in the Philippines, of course, followed MacArthur's advance closely and with so much interest because we were familiar with the places mentioned, and I am sure you have had the same interest in it as have we. Maybe MacArthur will clean up the Pacific War at the same time we finish over here. I hope both of them will be cleaned up soon, for I am homesick, and if my letters sound that way, you can be sure they are not deceiving you. I dream of that homecoming and long for it every day of my life over here.

I don't know how Paul Paschal got back home, but probably because he had been over here for so long a time. Many officers get run down and are sent back for a rest. Most of them are beginning to come back again, but I do not know if Paul is scheduled to return or not. I, too, am glad he wasn't reduced.[55]

Your letters were wonderful—they always are—and your Valentine was so sweet. I love you, darling, with all my heart and soul. Write often.

All my love and kisses to you and Tudy.
As ever, Always yours, Andy

Valentine's Day lifted the spirits of the troops fighting in the mud and rain of the Roer River and the approaches to the Schwammanauel Dam. This dam controlled the flow of water into the Roer. With an intact dam, the flow of water into the Roer was low, the waters calm, and the river narrow. With destruction of the dam, the rush of water would have been massive but temporary. Unfortunately for the Allies, the Germans destroyed the discharge valves, which resulted in a continuous flow of water that raised the Roer to flood levels that persisted for several weeks.

Immediate plans to clear the Lower Rhineland were thus delayed by the destruction of the discharge valves of the last uncaptured Roer dam on Bradley's front. The Canadian First Army, reinforced from the British Second Army, and the US Ninth Army were forced to fight along a narrow corridor through the Reichswald and across the Siegfried Line, opposed by eleven German divisions, half of them armored and composed of fanatical paratroopers determined to defend the fatherland and the increasingly precious Ruhr industrial area. Despite these troubles and concerns, the field marshal remained upbeat and visited frequently. After one such visit, to the XVI Corps headquarters, Field Marshal Montgomery expressed his thanks to General Anderson for sending him an XVI Corps patch.

The actions of Simpson's Ninth Army were beginning to attract the attention of the public. *Time* magazine published an article on February 19 detailing the buildup and preparations of the Ninth Army for the invasion of Germany. Simpson was featured on the cover of *Time*. His calm demeanor contrasted sharply in the public's eye with the aggressive personality of General Patton. Simpson was credited with running a "happy" headquarters where orders were given, resources made available, and cooperation in achieving the common goal of victory over the Germans was valued above all else.

Anderson and Simpson with One of Pat Echols' Friends on the Wall.

CHAPTER 9

XVI CORPS:
CROSSING THE ROER RIVER

FEBRUARY 1945

I t was back to business for the men of the US Ninth Army. It now consisted of three corps: the XIII, the XVI, and the XIX Corps. Each corps consisted of two divisions. Each division contained about 15,000 men. The Ninth Army attack codenamed "Operation Grenade" commenced on February 23 and was a three-corps effort to cross the Roer River and clear the approaches to the Rhine River by elimination of German resistance in the area between the two rivers.

Operation Grenade was primarily an all-United States effort. Gillem's XIII Corps and McLain's XIX Corps made the initial assault over the Roer. The XVI Corps was to provide coverage on the left flank of the XIII Corps. While the Roer was receding, it was still treacherous. The assault boats of the Thirtieth, Twenty-ninth, 102nd, and Eighty-fourth divisions swirled and twisted in the violent waters. Fighting the river as well as the enemy made for a difficult first day. Bridges were built over the Roer and decreased, but did not eliminate, the need for boat crossings. The Germans resisted furiously, including committing for the first time the ME-262 jet fighter-bomber to ground support operations.

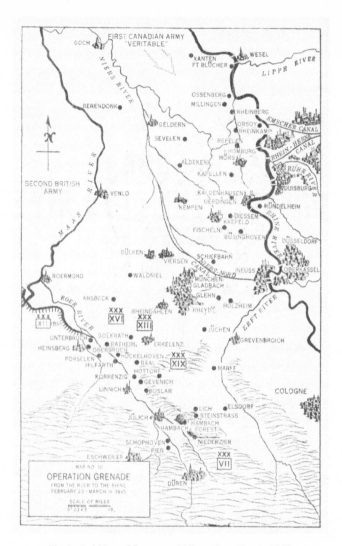

Illustrated Map of Roermond Liberation, March 1945

When the XIII and XIX Corps efforts in Operation Grenade stalled, Anderson's XVI Corps, initially held in reserve, moved forward. The XVI Corps, consisting of the Seventy-ninth and Thirty-fifth infantries, exploited a small gap in a very congested frontline. Anderson's men moved into the German lines and pressed ahead into a collapsing German line in leaps and bounds unexpected in the assault planning.

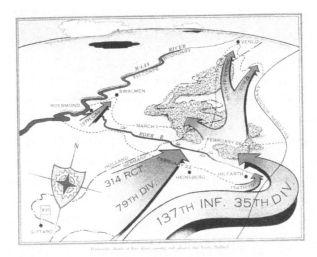

Illustrated Map of Roer River Crossing "by XVI Corps Units during Operation Grenade, 1945

Simpson praised the work of Anderson's men. He said, "Perhaps the outstanding event of Operation Grenade occurred when the XVI Corps sent a motorized task force, including the 320th Infantry Regiment of the 35th Division, and the 784th Tank Battalion, north all the way to Venlo." Venlo, bastion of the Siegfried Line and the impregnable Maas fortress, was taken from the rear without a fight. The once-mighty Panzer Lehr Division was committed to the effort but was unable to resist American mobility, power, and resources. On one occasion, an entire company of the Panzer Lehr Division, forced to fight as infantrymen, was captured, thinking they were in a reserve area near Munchen-Gladbach.

For the people of Roermond, on the other side of the Roer River, liberation arrived on March 1, 1945. On that day, the Recce Troop of the US Fifteenth Cavalry of the XVI Corps outflanked the Germans and forced them out of the city. Although the Germans had retreated and Roermond was spared house-to-house fighting, the city was still badly scarred with 90 percent of its buildings damaged or destroyed. The grateful people of Roermond welcomed their American liberators. Though Roermond was still mined and highly dangerous, the population turned out *en masse* to greet their American liberators.

Moving on from Roermond, the XVI Corps entered Germany. Fierce fighting continued but, as the next letter makes clear, there were some moments of levity, too. Famous actresses and pin-up girls were the subjects of both admiration and speculation. Marlene Dietrich raised quite a stir in the headquarters of the XVI Corps and its medical department.

March 4, 1945
Kaldenkirchen, Germany

My darling:

Received a nice, newsy long letter from you last evening.

The doctor who would not give Marlene[56] a cold shot in the hip was Doc Simmons of my Headquarters Company. He got a lot of kidding when the story got out. But the story is true. Marlene, who was to have had lunch at my mess one noon, never did arrive, as I told you in an earlier letter. I didn't see her while she was in the area.

Preparations were now underway for the Rhine River crossing. The Americans and British were building up a huge force under Field Marshal Montgomery's command for a set-piece assault over the Rhine. American generals not involved in the operation were increasingly jealous and irritated. Generals Patton and Bradley were particularly resentful of resources demanded and the attention being paid to Montgomery.

March 5, 1945
Kaldenkirchen,[57] Germany

My darling:

The secrecy ban on the XVI Corps and two of my three divisions was lifted today, so I now can tell you that I have the 35th Infantry Division, commanded by Paul Baade, and the 8th Armored Division, commanded by Johnny Devine. The third division has not been released as yet. I had a fourth division for a time but it was shifted to another corps. It too has been released so I can tell you that that was Billy Wyche's 79th. It took part in our initial attack, but only with our regiment and the division artillery. Of course, we are all in the Ninth Army, and we think it is the best army on the western front. The 35th Division is a veteran outfit and a splendid division. They have done a swell job. The 8th Armored is new but they have also done exceedingly well.

We liberated Venlo and Roermond in Holland and then turned to the northeast. We made contact with the British and Canadians coming down from the north, and have now pushed on toward the Rhine. My first elements reached the Rhine a couple of hours ago. Venlo's capture by the 35th Division was quite a spectacular operation, and though not receiving much publicity, was one of the longest and speediest advances made by any unit in this operation. The Dutch there had been under the Germans for almost five years and they went wild when our troops entered the city. The 35th, who had also taken part in the liberation of France, said the excitement and gratitude of the people in Venlo exceeded anything they had encountered in France.

Hope our success in driving the krauts across the Rhine will shorten the war, but it appears as though we'll have to cross that river and continue the destruction of the German army before peace will come in Europe. Hope we can speed that day.

All my love and kisses to you, precious, and to Tudy.

As ever, Always yours. Andy

March 6, 1945
Kaldenkirchen, Germany

My darling:

This has been a day of many visitors, the most important was Simp. He is always welcome for he is a grand commander and we all are so fond of him and appreciate his human attitude and his ability.

The Field Marshal Montgomery sent me a personal message today thanking the Corps for our assistance to the British and Canadian forces to our north. It was quite complimentary, but was delivered orally by one of his liaison officers so I have no record of it to send to you and Tudy. However, I appreciate the message nevertheless.

Always yours, Andy

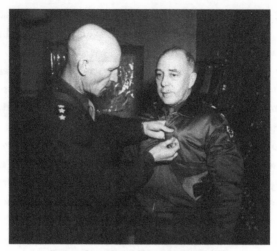

Bronze Star Medal Presentation, 1945

During General Simpson's visit, Simpson presented Anderson a Bronze Star medal. The presentation ceremony took place at a time of an increasing tempo of Ninth Army actions with planning for the Rhine River crossing consuming most every moment. Wearing his service .45 automatic pistol, Anderson received the award dressed in combat boots, leggings, and jacket in a map room with little ceremony and few others in attendance. The award was a nice early birthday present.

March 11, 1945
Nieukirk, Germany

My darling:

Had as nice a birthday as I could have without being with you and Tudy. In addition to the birthday cake from the mess personnel, and presents of cigarettes from Tarsay and Huegge and Charles at noon, last evening the staff assembled to greet me at a cocktail party. The cocktails were rather limited and consisted mostly of the presents that were brought to me which were, 1 bottle of Scotch, 3 bottles of champagne, and 4 bottles of wine, including what Charles Busbee sent me. But all of us at least had one drink apiece, and above all, I appreciated the fine spirit of all those present. I feel that I have the most loyal staff that anyone could ask for.

Today I had a telegram from Omar Bradley who apparently had checked on my birthday. I think it was a fine gesture and extremely thoughtful of him.

All my love and kisses to you and Tudy, As ever, Always yours, Andy

CHAPTER 10

XVI CORPS: CROSSING THE RHINE RIVER

MARCH 1945

C ommand of the XVI Corps was the most important command
of Anderson's career. The culmination of his time in the service
was the assignment to lead the XVI Corps attack across the
Rhine River as the tip of the spear of Simpson's Ninth Army.

Anderson's letter this date gives only a small hint of the
monumental events building toward the crossing of the Rhine. He
does refer to the fact that General George Patton was "in the news"
and praises his efforts to destroy the German army.

March 23, 1945
Lintfort, Germany

My darling:

We have had about five days of almost ideal spring weather. We
are all enjoying it for more reasons than the mere fact that it is
beautiful weather. Unquestionably, it is helping us to speed the final
defeat of the krauts. The air efforts during these beautiful days has

been tremendous, and, of course, it is also helping our ground efforts in the First, Third and Seventh Army fronts. Georgie Patton certainly has been going to town again with his army. We do not know just what his score is, but unquestionably he has destroyed a nice sized section of the German army.

Must close now as I have a busy day laid out. All my love and kisses to you, my darling, and to Tudy. As ever, Always yours, Andy

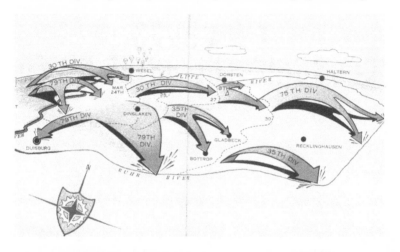

Illustrated Map of Units of the XVI Corps in Rhine Crossing

The main assault across the Rhine began that day. Planning had begun in January 1945. Final details were agreed upon on March 21 during Anderson's visit to the Ninth Army command post in Munchen-Gladbach. No detail was left to chance. Overwhelming force, extensive artillery preparation, and combined air and land assault were planned to give the greatest chance of success. The assault over the Rhine was one of the most ambitious inland amphibious operations ever conceived. As commander of the Twenty-first Army Group consisting of the US Ninth Army, the British Second Army, and the Canadian First Army, Field Marshal Montgomery had at his disposal forces totaling more than a million men in twenty-nine divisions and, like the Normandy landings, the attack across the Rhine was a joint United States, British, and Canadian effort. The combined operation was code-named "Operation Plunder."

Anderson's XVI Corps was given the assignment of directing and leading the American effort. The Ninth Army's assault was code-named "Operation Flashpoint." With this assignment came a remarkable buildup of men and resources. Five divisions (the Thirtieth, Seventy-ninth, Seventy-fifth, and Thirty-fifth and the Eighth Armored) and supporting artillery units increased the XVI Corps to the size of an army.

The XVI Corps artillery commander, Brigadier General Charles C. Brown, was responsible not only for his own corps artillery but also the Thirty-fourth Field Artillery Brigade under Brigadier General John F. Uncles with its thirteen battalions of medium, heavy, and superheavy artillery pieces. The XIX Corps artillery under Brigadier General George D. Shea with eleven battalions of artillery joined the XVI Corps. A total of more than 2,000 artillery pieces were under XVI Corps command for the destruction of German targets. Tank destroyer battalions, antiaircraft artillery groups, and smoke/chemical units were added, bringing the total number of men under Anderson's command to 120,000, more an army than a corps.[58] This concentration of power was the largest corps command in Europe during the Second World War.

Eisenhower (left) and Anderson (right) at Ease Before Rhine River Crossing with Colonel Barkley (center) at XVI Corps Headquarters, March 24, 1945.

During the evening of March 23, Generals Eisenhower and Simpson visited XVI Corps headquarters at Lintfort to prepare for the upcoming visit of Prime Minister Winston Churchill, Chief of the Imperial General Staff Sir Alanbrooke, and Field Marshal

Montgomery to observe the attack over the Rhine. During the course of the evening, Eisenhower reminded those present that Churchill could be impetuous and would likely try to cross the Rhine. He reiterated his concern repeatedly about the foolishness of allowing the prime minister to attempt to join the troops and cross the Rhine on the day of attack.

The attack over the Rhine began with a diversionary assault away from the main attack point, by the British Army Fifty-first Highland Division and First Commando Brigade at Rees, downstream and to the north of the main attack point. The diversionary attack kicked off the evening of March 23.

General Anderson Gives Order to Artillery Chief of Section to Fire First Rounds Over the Rhine, Operation Flashpoint and Grenade, Rheinberg, Germany, March 24, 1945

Beginning at one a.m. on March 24, 1945, the artillery opened up. By virtue of the fact that the land west of the Rhine was flat, and there was a three-quarters moon, every cannon shot was visible to Generals Eisenhower, Simpson, and Anderson from their observation post in the town of Rheinberg. Artillery rounds arched over their heads. In the first hour, more than 1,000 rounds were fired each minute. Sited carefully on predetermined targets, the effect was devastating on the German defenders. Over the next four hours, the onslaught of artillery fire continued with more than 218,000 rounds ranging from twenty-five pounds to 325 pounds raining down on the east side of the Rhine and the German army.

The main attack by the US Thirtieth and Seventy-ninth infantry divisions began under cover of darkness and smoke screens during the wee hours of the 24th. First assault boats, then landing crafts carried infantrymen over the Rhine. Soon, the east bank of the Rhine was secured and pontoon bridges put in place. Trucks, tanks, and field artillery followed the men over these bridges, rapidly expanding the bridgehead.

At dawn on the 24th, the daylight airborne assault by the First Allied Airborne Army, code-named "Operation Varsity," included the US XVII Airborne Division and the British Sixth Airborne Division. Operation Varsity was the largest and last paratrooper assault of the war. More than 16,000 men jumped from more than 1,500 transport aircraft. Others arrived via the more than 1,350 gliders. The airborne armada stretched out over 200 miles and lasted more than two and a half hours. More than 2,500 men died in this assault.

On March 25, Anderson took time to write his wife a few lines. This letter gives intimate details of the events of the crossing and the pivotal role played by the men of the XVI Corps.

March 25, 1945
Lintfort, Germany

My darling:

The secrecy on what we are doing has been removed, so what I tell you will probably be old news long before this reaches you. Yesterday morning the XVI Corps crossed the Rhine. We were the only Ninth Army troops involved in the crossing, the remainder being British troops. Everything went off according to plan and we have a very substantial bridgehead on the other side now. I was on the east bank for a short while this afternoon when we took the Prime Minister across in a boat.

Ike and Simp came up and spent Friday night with me—that was the night we crossed—and we all stayed up to see the artillery preparation which lasted from one to three. They left yesterday after lunch, but returned today for lunch. In addition, Bradley, Field Marshal Montgomery and Winston Churchill came for lunch today, and afterward we took all of them to a point on the Rhine where they could see our pontoon bridges and from where we took them over the Rhine in a landing craft. It has been a busy two days, and now that all the important visitors have been here and gone, I can devote a little more time to fighting the war.

My two assault divisions have been released. They are Billy Wyche's 79th and Leland Hobbs's 30th. They have done a wonderful job and are still going. I have three more divisions which should be over or partially over within the next day or two. Hope we'll be well on our way, or in, Berlin by the time this reaches you. Ordinarily, I am not too optimistic, but I really believe the end of the European war is definitely in sight.

All my love and kisses to you, my darling, and to Tudy. Tell Tudy I'll write her and enclose some autographs soon.

As ever, Always yours, Andy

Simpson, Anderson, and Bradley speak with Field Marshal Montgomery and Sir Alanbrooke (behind Montgomery) Awaiting Winston Churchill's Arrival, West Bank of the Rhine, March 25, 1945.

Major General Anderson hosted a remarkable group on Sunday morning, March 25, 1945. All principal members of the Allied war effort in northern Europe at the time of the Rhine River crossing were present. Prior to the arrival of their British guests, Generals Simpson and Anderson reviewed the overall situation and the progress being made by the assault divisions. That morning, their British guests attended Palm Sunday services in Venlo. Sir Alanbrooke gave this account of the morning's activity:

"The hymns were good, and the parson, a Presbyterian, preached a good sermon. After church, we motored off to Rheinberg, where Anderson, commanding the American XVI Corps, had his H.Q. We were met there by Eisenhower, Bradley and Simpson."[59]

Shortly thereafter, Churchill arrived at the headquarters of the XVI Corps at Rheinberg.

Anderson and Simpson Talking with Prime Minister Winston Churchill Before Rhine River Crossing, March 25, 1945.

After all the arrivals, briefings, and greetings, the party enjoyed a luncheon of fried chicken, sandwiches, potato salad, and cake. Churchill enjoyed his usual whiskey and soda, discreetly disposing of his glass behind a convenient telephone pole.

Churchill Is Now Ready For the Day's Activity, Crossing the Rhine.

A firsthand account of the events of the day was published by *Chicago Tribune* correspondent Henry Wales.[60] He had been invited by Major "Barney" Oldfield, in charge of the Ninth Army press camp, to report on the events.

"From a second-floor balcony, Churchill stared across the Rhine and remarked, 'The last time I was on the Rhine was in the Cologne bridgehead after the last war, when we cruised 50 miles up the river in a British gunboat. I should very much like to go across.'

"Eisenhower shook his head in response to this request to 'get across.' So too did Monty [Field Marshal Bernard Law Montgomery, Viscount of Alamein, commanding general of the Twenty-first Army Group]."

Eisenhower was clear in his directive to deny Churchill this opportunity to go forward. The prime minister was described as "having the face of a disappointed school boy." But he was not to be denied.

Eisenhower and Bradley departed. Eisenhower headed for Paris and the Raphael Hotel.[61] Noting Eisenhower's departure, Henry Wales reported, *"After his departure Churchill coaxed General Anderson into agreeing to the excursion."* They were headed across the Rhine.

How did the Prime Minister convince Anderson to do his bidding? Did Churchill remember their meeting the previous September and recall their conversations aboard the *Queen Mary* or did he invoke the memory of doughboys and Tommies together in the trenches of Flanders? Anderson was likely genuinely sympathetic to the Prime Minister's request despite Eisenhower's disapproval. But Eisenhower had made his desires known that Churchill be restricted from crossing the Rhine. Could Anderson resist the charm and wheedling of Churchill? Apparently not. For although we will never know exactly what was said, we do know that Churchill soon clambered aboard a US Navy landing craft with his entourage and was off for the eastern shore of the Rhine.

Winston Churchill & Entourage Crossing The Rhine, March 25 1945

Correspondent Henry Wales continued with his own account of events: *"Churchill was the first ashore on the east bank of the Rhine. A couple of Yanks were playing catch and the Prime Minister climbed atop the first dike and started toward a village a mile away. 'This area is not entirely swept of mines,' warned General Anderson. Monty was worried and convinced Churchill to abandon his promenade. Even the debonair General Simpson showed concern as Churchill clambered on the girders of the demolished Wesel Bridge.*

"Several cracks and pings were heard and Military Policeman Private Larry Kelly of Cleveland, Ohio, pointed out the 'Jerry' snipers being cleaned out by some of our fellows. Private James Fortuin of Chicago pointed out 'the boys snaking along by that busted church? They're mopping up.' Moments later, four detonations followed by a quartet of geysers 50 feet high erupted in the middle of the river, evenly spaced, with the nearest about 50 yards from the bridge upon which Churchill perched. Staff Sgt. James Scott of Chicago warned the party to take cover as two more shells landed in the fields 100 yards behind the group. Montgomery and Simpson abandoned diplomatic language and insisted the party return across the Rhine."

And so, the party returned to the landing craft and departed for the west bank of the Rhine. Although only one of hundreds of slow-gaited landing craft and small naval ships supporting the rapid expansion of the Ninth Army beachhead on the east side of the Rhine, this craft contained Prime Minister Churchill; the Chief of the Imperial War Staff, Sir Alanbrooke; the Commanding General of the Twenty-first Army Group, Field Marshal Montgomery; the Commanding General of the US Ninth Army, William H. Simpson; the Commanding General of the US XVI Corps, John B. Anderson, and the Commanding General of the US Thirtieth Infantry Division, Leland S. Hobbs.

Eisenhower's concerns were understandable. In one small vessel, a landing craft with thin steel sides unable to withstand shell splinters, bullets, or mortar fire, were the heads of the British government, British military, and all British ground forces in Europe. With one well-placed or lucky round, a crisis of full measure could have ensued should Churchill, Alanbrooke, and Montgomery have been wounded or killed.

Meanwhile, the loss of three American generals would have paled in comparison to the loss of these men who carried such a great weight of responsibility for the British war effort. If Simpson, Anderson, and Hobbs had been killed, the American war effort would have hardly skipped a beat. To put the potential loss of the British occupants of this landing craft in perspective, imagine the consequences to the American war effort if President Franklin Roosevelt, Army Chief of Staff George Marshall, and General Dwight Eisenhower had been shot down and killed while flying together!

Fortunately, everyone returned safely—no loss of life and no loss of momentum as the Rhine River crossing continued unabated. The photograph taken the morning of March 25, 1945, electrified the public and boosted the Allied war effort. For the American high commanders Dwight Eisenhower and Omar Bradley, the reaction was different. Their absence from the photo suggested that the British were in command of the Rhine River crossing and were responsible for the bulk of the manpower and resources for the crossing. Nothing could be further from the truth.

Upon learning of Churchill's crossing the Rhine, Eisenhower later said, "Had I been present, he would never have been permitted to cross the Rhine that day."[62] Was he worried about Churchill's safety or that the spotlight was put on Churchill and the British contingent with whom he had argued so long and so hard? We will likely never know. We do know that Eisenhower felt the press paid inordinate attention to Montgomery. We also know that Bradley was especially sensitive to the attention paid to his English rival.

Alanbrooke also reacted to the photo. Two days later, he observed in a letter to his wife, Lady Brookeborough, that Churchill "was determined to take every risk he could possibly take and, if possible, endanger his life to the maximum! I rather feel that he considers a sudden and soldierly death at the front, to die fighting with your blood up, would be a suitable ending to his famous life and would free him from the never-ending worries which loom ahead with our Russian friends and others." [63]

Regardless of any controversy surrounding the photo and the trip across the Rhine, Anderson's XVI Corps advanced quickly and in depth. Progress was unabated. Over the next three days, the US Thirty-fifth Division joined in and advanced to attack Gladbeck and Bottrop. The US Eighth Armored Division completed its move over the Rhine. By the end of March 28, XVI Corps strength on the east bank of the Rhine was three infantry divisions (the Thirtieth, Thirty-fifth, and Seventy-ninth), an armored division (the Eighth), and nine field artillery battalions. Anderson moved XVI Corps headquarters forward, over the Rhine, to be as close to the front as possible. Total XVI Corps casualties for the crossing of the Rhine were 154 missing or captured, 2,079 wounded, and 291 killed. German casualties were 1,342 killed and 9,095 captured.

March 29, 1945
Letkampshof, Germany

My darling:

I haven't written you for two days as I have been quite busy, including a move of my headquarters. We are now east of the Rhine. This is our fourth headquarters location in Germany, all the moves having been made in less than a month. We seem to be on your way to Berlin at last.

Brad sent me a nice note today, which I am enclosing. He is such a fine fellow, in every respect, and I admire him, particularly for his modesty and unassuming attitude. He was among my many visitors last Sunday, whom I told you about. I'll repeat them, however, in case that letter miscarried. They were: Prime Minister Churchill, Montgomery, Eisenhower, Bradley, Simpson, and Field Marshal Brooke. Many smaller fry also. Other visitors during the early phases of the Rhine crossing were very numerous, of course, among the most prominent being Air Marshal Tedder of the British Air Forces. Ike and Simp visited me twice, spending D-day [64]night and most of D-day with me.

You asked me in your letter the names of the locations at which the Corps had been before we entered Germany. I can now tell you where we were. In Normandy, we were in Barneville; in Belgium, we were in Tongres, and in Holland we were at two places, first at Heerlen and lastly at Sittard. We jumped from Sittard to our first location in Germany. You also asked who had the XIX Corps before McLain. The former commander was Pete Corlett, who went home sick. I understand he has now recovered and has Andy's corps, and Andy has the replacement center at Sill. It would appear from this change that Andy will not again be sent overseas. [The Andy referred to here is Jonathan W. Anderson, who preceded "Cowboy Pete" Corlett as Commanding General of the XXXVI Corps].

The war seems to be going very well for us on all fronts over here. I cannot understand why the krauts keep on fighting. It is remarkable how Hitler has instilled a fanatical spirit into these people to the extent of fighting to the death and watching their towns and cities being reduced to heaps of rubble by our air and artillery. You cannot begin to realize the total destruction of these German towns we are passing through.

Must close now, darling. All my love and kisses to you and Tudy.

As ever, Always yours, Andy

March 29, 1945
Letkampshof, Germany

Dearest Tudy:
I know you must have had a grand time at West Point on the 100th Night weekend. And I see that Johnny Chickering[65] has come into the

picture again, and has asked you to come up for a weekend. I suppose there were thrills for you, when that invitation came through! Haven't seen Stan for about two months, although we haven't been very far removed from each other. Of course, we have both been rather busy working on the krauts.

I still have Tommy Donaldson[66] in one of my divisions. He is a mighty fine boy, I think, and is doing a fine job in his assignment.

All my love and kisses, dearest, to you and mother.

As ever, Your daddy

So, despite all the responsibilities of command of the XVI Corps, Anderson had the time and inclination to look out for and report on the activities of young men interested in his daughter.

April 6, 1945
Letkampshof, Germany

My precious darling:

No, Simp did not take the responsibility for letting Churchill cross the Rhine. The old man wanted to cross on the pontoon bridge, but I protested as the bridge was working at capacity and Churchill's party was so big it would add an unnecessary burden. So, I appealed to Simp and he in turn appealed to Ike, who said "No!" After Ike and Bradley left, the old man saw one of our LCMs going across and asked if he could cross that way, and Marshall Montgomery said he saw no objection. That is the story of the crossing. The old man was determined to get across, one way or another, however.

Write often, darling. All my love and kisses to you and Tudy.

As ever, Always yours, Andy

So, here is another firsthand account of the decision to cross the Rhine with Churchill. Because Anderson was in control of all the tactical resources in the area—the boats and trucks and bridges—it would have likely been his decision to summon the LCM landing craft to the west bank of the Rhine. Although Montgomery offered no objection, the final decision was Anderson's and his alone.

CHAPTER 11

XVI CORPS: RUHR POCKET REDUCTION AND SURRENDER

APRIL-MAY 1945

The crossing of the Rhine by the XVI Corps occurred at Wesel, Germany, immediately north of the industrial Ruhr area. Simpson's Ninth Army XIII and XIX Corps followed the XVI Corps over the Rhine. The XIII and XIX Corps raced east toward Berlin. The XVI Corps was assigned the task of attacking the northern half of the Ruhr pocket. The Ruhr was the industrial heartland of Germany and essential for the German's continued resistance. Without the Ruhr industries, the Germans could no longer fight. As such, the Ruhr was well defended both in terms of men and fortresses. To attack the Ruhr area head-on would have been suicidal. Another way had to be found to neutralize this vital German resource.

After the Rhine River crossing, the Ninth Army reverted to Bradley's Twelfth Army Group from Montgomery's Twenty-first Army Group. General Bradley decided to use with Anderson's XVI Corps of Simpson's Ninth Army and J. Lawton Collin's VII Corps and Van Fleet's III Corps of Hodges' First Army to encircle the Ruhr. All three corps involved in the operation were heavily reinforced for the difficult urban warfare and house-to-house fighting. The reduction of the Ruhr pocket was strictly an American affair.

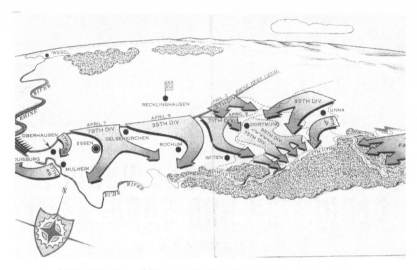

Illustrated Map of Ruhr Pocket Reduction from the North, 1945

Anderson's XVI headquarters coordinated the attacks of the Eighth Armored Division, the Seventeenth Airborne Division, and the Ninety-fifth, Thirty-fifth, Seventy-ninth, and Seventy-fifth infantry divisions north of the Ruhr River to capture the towns of Oberhausen, Mulheim, Gelsenkirchen, Bochum, Witten, Dortmund, and Unna. These vital industrial areas between the Rhine-Herne Canal and the Ruhr River deprived the Germans of essential war-making material and were fiercely defended with Tiger tanks, especially in the Unna/ Dortmund area. Although intelligence reports had estimated the German forces in the Ruhr pocket at 150,000 men, in fact, the total number of Germans ultimately captured was more than 315,000. German losses during the Ruhr pocket reduction resulted in the end of any effective resistance by German forces in the west.

It was later revealed during the interrogation of Lieutenant General Fritz Bayerlein, the commanding general of the German LIII Corps and former commander of the German Panzer Lehr Division, that orders from Field Marshal Walther Model to break out of the Ruhr pocket were deemed unrealistic and ignored. Model, the commander of the German forces in the Ruhr pocket, refused to surrender. He believed that no field marshal should ever surrender. He felt a field marshal should commit suicide instead of being captured. True to his beliefs, when he concluded that he was soon to be captured, he walked into a forest and shot himself.

On April 10, 1945, the industrial city of Essen, with the sprawling Krupp Steel Works, fell to the combined forces under XVI Corps command. Although 200 miles to the west of Berlin, the loss of Essen and the Ruhr Valley on April 10 effectively ended the war in the west.

Far removed from the fight, General Bradley said "all the German forces surrendered without a fight."[67] Closer to the front and its realities, General Anderson described it as "a mean job."

April 10, 1945
Recklinghausen, Germany

My precious:

Had a sweet letter from you last evening, mailed on March 25, but due to a busy day, I did not get a letter to you. I had to visit two newly acquired divisions and I am now covering so wide a front I can only reach all of it by taking a day for each half of it. I at present have six divisions and every one working. Hope to peel off a few in a day or so, however.

The report about Van Pope being a major general is incorrect, as he is still with the 86th Division as assistant division commander. By the way, I saw a list of new generals the other day which included Jimmy Lester and Lew Pick as major generals.[68]

I do not believe the papers at home indicated that the XVI Corps was the only part of the Ninth Army which crossed the Rhine on D-day. We spear-headed the army attack and after we had established a deep enough bridgehead, the other two corps followed us over and then spread out to the north flank. So, we really had the honor spot, so to speak, in the crossing. I feel we did a good job, and, above all, quickly drove in our bridgehead with a very minimum of casualties.

All my love and kisses to you, my darling, and to Tudy.

As ever, always yours, Andy

President Franklin Roosevelt died on April 12, 1945, and was succeeded as president by Harry S. Truman of Missouri. No mention of this event is made in Anderson's letters.

April 15, 1945
Recklinghausen, Germany

My darling:

The 8th Armored seems to have gotten a lot of credit for many things they didn't do, judging from what you said in the sweet letter I received from you last night, mailed on March 31st. As I have told you before, the 30th and 79th, followed by the 35th, all infantry divisions, did the big job in crossing the Rhine and expanding the bridgehead. I brought over the 8th Armored several days after the crossing and they did hit the 116th Panzer, but didn't get far and I finally had to put in another infantry division, the 75th, to break that deadlock. No reflection on the 8th, particularly, for, after all, the kind of fighting they were up against required an infantry division rather than an armored.

My divisions in the reduction of the Ruhr pocket have now been announced, so I can tell you what they were. I had as high as seven divisions for this job—the 17th Airborne, the 79th, 75th, 35th, 95th, 29th Infantry Divisions and the 8th Armored. We captured Essen and Dortmund and cleared all the northern part of the Ruhr area. Since the job is now completed, I have lost the 8th Armored and the 35th, and am due to lose the 75th and 29th soon. It was a mean job. In the course of the operation we captured Von Papen,[69] his son and son-in-law. I referred to this experience in a letter a few days ago, and said I'd tell you about it as soon as it was released, which release took place today.

Again, my precious, all my love on the occasion of our 21st wedding anniversary and wish I could be with you. I love you and you have made the last 21 years the best years of my life.

Write often, precious. All my love and kisses to you and Tudy. As ever, Always yours, Andy

Captured High-Ranking German Industrialist Alfred Krupp and former German Chancellor Franz von Papen.

Another important captive of the XVI Corps was Alfred Krupp von Bohlen, an industrialist who owned the Krupp Steel Works in Essen. Krupp used slave labor from concentration camps in his many factories. For this crime against humanity, he was convicted and sentenced to twelve years in prison and forfeiture of all personal property. After three years, he was pardoned and his property was returned.

April 17, 1945
Recklinghausen, Germany

My darling:

Can't say I have enjoyed "pal"-ing with the big shots. I always heave a sigh of relief when they are gone. They take so much of one's time, because you have to pay attention to them, and time is never plentiful enough to do all the things we have to do, especially during operations. And, of course, it is during the most active phase of an operation when they show up.

We hadn't realized over here that there had been so much discussion about who was to head the invasion of Japan. The Stars and Stripes has not mentioned the matter nor have our radio broadcasts had anything to say about it. When Gen. Pennell[70] was here he said it had been occupying headlines and radio newscasts for some time, and had aroused much bitter discussion and criticism at home. Well at last it has been settled, according to your letter last night, and I am delighted that MacArthur is to retain command.

As ever, Always yours, Andy

After the reduction of the Ruhr pocket, Anderson had an opportunity to rest and reflect upon the achievements of the XVI Corps. He was undoubtedly aware of the drama being played out to the east involving the rest of Simpson's Ninth Army sitting on the Elbe River.

In an unprecedented act, on March 28, 1945, Eisenhower communicated directly with Soviet Premier Josef Stalin and stated that United States forces would stop at the Elbe River.

By mid-April, the Ninth Army was resting on the west bank of the Elbe with an established bridgehead on the eastern shore, ready to press on to Berlin. The American Army had always considered Berlin the goal of the war in the west. All of the major Allies—British, American, and Russian—wanted to be the first military force into the German capital. The United States, the Soviet Union, and England all felt they had legitimate claims to the German capitol. The United States had the most powerful army with the most powerful weapons in its army and air forces; the Russians had captured and killed more German soldiers; and the British had fought longer and alone in the most desperate circumstances. Each country's political leadership wanted to be the first to Berlin. Thus, each officer and soldier were motivated by the press and the public to carry on the fight to the end in Berlin.

Churchill understood better than almost anyone else that the capture of Berlin would have significant consequences in post-war Europe. He stated time and again that the ambitions of Stalin and the Soviet Union were to dominate post-war Europe. Whoever occupied Berlin would be in a position of great strength and power to signal to the rest of the world its dominance. At the Yalta Conference in early February 1945, Churchill tried in vain to impress upon Roosevelt the danger of giving Stalin too much leeway in the division of Europe in the post-war era. Unfortunately, Roosevelt was too ill to fight back against Stalin's increasing demands.

Churchill felt Eisenhower had seriously overstepped his authority. He was not pleased at the naiveté of the American commanders who seemed to think it was their responsibility to abide by the political agreements of the Tehran and Yalta conferences rather than focus on their country's immediate military objectives. In *A Soldier's Story*,[71] General Bradley was to write later, "As soldiers we looked naively on the British inclination to complicate the war with political foresight and nonmilitary objectives." General Marshall demanded an explanation. Eisenhower said, "Berlin is only a political objective, not a military objective."

Eisenhower's motive most likely was an effort to avoid unnecessary casualties and the need to "give land back to the Soviets" in order to comply with the Tehran Conference accords. Omar Bradley had estimated that 100,000 casualties would be incurred taking Berlin.

Bradley's casualty estimate served as one of the main factors that Eisenhower relied on to abandon the plan to go to Berlin and stop at the Elbe. However, both Patton of the Third Army and Simpson of the Ninth Army pressed Bradley and Eisenhower in person for permission to continue on to Berlin. On April 11, the Ninth Army already had two bridgeheads over the Elbe. In fact, Joseph C. Harsch, a reporter for the *Christian Science Monitor*, recalls that on April 14, 1945, reporters with the Ninth Army "rode in jeeps to the outskirts of Berlin without incident or obstruction."

On or about April 12, 1945, Eisenhower ordered US Army forces to "stand on the Elbe." His decision to stop at the Elbe River was the most controversial one of his military career. Reflecting later on Eisenhower's decision, Bradley wrote, "We probably could have pushed on to Berlin."

They were forbidden to press on. For nearly a month, the Ninth Army sat on the west bank of the Elbe with little to do.

Anderson's letters home do not hint of the existence nor the magnitude of this controversy. His responsibility was increasingly that of boosting the morale of the men under his command, the care and feeding of displaced persons in refugee camps all over the United States zone of occupation, and the disposition of troops anxious to return home.

5 May, 1945
Beckum, Germany

My darling:

In my last letter, written on the second, I said I knew I'd miss a letter to you on the 3rd as I had to go to Army on that day, but I didn't expect to miss two days. But yesterday I had an important civilian visitor, the same one who came to Riley for dinner one evening last June. He spent the whole day with me, and I think enjoyed himself.[72]

Patton and Hodges will remain in their present assignments. Their promotion is a partial attempt to give the proper rank which goes with their jobs. Army commanders are supposed to be four-star generals, corps commanders three stars, and divisions, two stars. I understand two or three corps commanders, including Ham Haislip,[73] have been made lieutenant generals.[74] I do not know how far they will carry this idea through, but sincerely hope Simp will get his fourth star—he certainly deserves it, as, of course, does Patch.

Yes, I saw Von Papen and his son and son-in-law. Had a short conversation with the old man, who, of course, speaks excellent English. He wouldn't talk much, but gave Gen. Simpson and myself both the impression that he was in bad with the Nazis and was quite relieved to be safely in American hands. I don't know what has happened to him.

My divisions have changed again, but at present I have four. Since they are all off the secret list, I can tell you that they are the 75th, 79th, 95th, and 29th. I recently lost the 35th and 17th Airborne. I certainly have had a parade of divisions in the past two months, or less time for that matter.

Always yours, Andy

May 7, 1945
Beckum, Germany

My darling:

At present, I am temporary "governor" of a section of Germany about the size of New Jersey. I say temporary because this is in a section of Germany that is eventually to be occupied by the British. I do not know what troops are to remain in the American army of occupation, but feel reasonably sure it will not include the XVI Corps.

How soon we might be sent home, or elsewhere, I do not know, but if it should be home I'd be willing to sit by and wait patiently for our turn. We should be learning something definite before many days have passed.

Must go out and award a medal to one of my men. I love you, darling.

As ever, Always yours, Andy

CHAPTER 12

XVI CORPS TRIUMPHANT

MAY 1945

Sue "Tudy" Moore Anderson, my mother and General Anderson's daughter, wrote to her father on May 7, 1945, the day the German Army surrendered. The war was over!

Dearest Daddy,   May 7, 1945

It is hard to believe but apparently V-E Day has finally arrived! The things I feel are impossible to put into words—but I want you to know that my main thought is, and has been from the moment I heard the news, that now you'll be coming home! You know that, like you, I've never been able to really express how I feel but, Daddy, it's been so lonesome

without you—and I've missed you more than you'll ever know! We had a lovely, if tearful, chapel service this morning (they generously (?) gave us a free period too) and we went to church tonight. Mother got a nervous reaction and had to leave the latter. You can imagine what her trouble was!

We're all so grateful and thankful that it's over! You've fought a <u>wonderful</u> fight so now—please come home!

Sue 'Tudy' Moore
Anderson, May, 1945.

See you soon—All my love, yours, Tudy

May 8, 1945
Beckum, Germany

My darling:

Everyone, according to the radio, appears to be celebrating today as VE Day, although it has not been announced officially as yet.

Jascha Heifetz[75] is playing concerts for the troops in the corps. I haven't heard him play as yet, but hope I'll be able to find time to attend one of his concerts before he leaves the area. He and his accompanist are to have lunch with us at my mess this noon. I haven't met him as yet, but he is due to arrive here at my office in a few minutes. If he arrives before I finish this letter, I'll give you my impressions.

Tomorrow we are having a parade and official announcement of VE Day. We are having a band and a battalion from one of the divisions put on the parade. The program includes prayers of thanks by the three corps chaplains—Protestant, Catholic, and Jewish—and the playing of the national anthems of England, Russia, France and the U.S. We couldn't play the national anthems of all the United Nations without exhausting the band, I suppose. The formation is intended to impress the Germans with the fact they have been defeated, as well as its celebration purpose for ourselves.

As ever, Always yours, Andy

General Anderson was now free to give details of events. Spartan living conditions, anxiety about the possibility of further service in the Pacific or a longer stay in the Occupation Army in Germany, and exhaustion with the crushing weight of command are all apparent as he pours out the pent-up emotions of more than eight months in the field.

May 20, 1945
Beckum, Germany

My darling:

It is eight months ago today that we sailed from New York, and almost nine since I left you and Tudy in Staunton. It seems like at least eight years. And so much has happened in those eight months that I hardly know where to begin in describing what has taken place.

As you already know, we landed at Gourock, Scotland, and were whisked to Southampton overnight, loaded on landing craft the following day, and the day after that landed in Normandy. Our headquarters were at Barneville on the ocean, directly opposite Guernsey Island, which was reputed to be held by 15,000-20,000 Germans. I never have heard just how many were on the island when it finally surrendered on VE Day (Reybold just told me there were 25,000 Germans on the islands, including Jersey as well as Guernsey). The island is about 12 to 15 miles offshore, and looked to be much closer than that. We had to protect the peninsula against raids from this island, but the two months we were there, they gave us no trouble. A couple of months ago they did make a raid on the peninsula, but it didn't amount to much. In addition, we had the mission of gathering up new units when they arrived, seeing to it that they were equipped and then shipping them off to the different armies. It was here that I first saw the 102nd and the only time I have had it under my command, and then only for a couple of days.

Barneville was the most unpleasant place climatically that we have been. There was a great shortage of fuel and so we were not physically comfortable either. We also had to confine ourselves to definite restricted areas because of the many minefields the Germans had planted along the coast in their defense systems. There were quite a number of casualties among the troops from this cause, despite all our efforts to warn them upon their arrival of the danger. We lost one truck in headquarters but fortunately had no personnel causalities. The troops, for the most part, had to live in pup tents in fields of mud, but that could not be avoided as there were not enough billets to even begin to house all the troops passing through. We had as many as four divisions at one time, in addition to numberless artillery, tank, tank destroyer, medical, quartermaster and all other types of units. It was a thankless job and we were glad to leave the place which we did on November 28, two months to the day, from our arrival.

The people were friendly but not enthusiastic by any manner of means. They are the stolid peasant type, of course, and also the first flush of liberation had begun to pall by the time we got there. There were several instances of sniping while we were there, which may have been either French Nazi sympathizers or escaped German POWs. We never caught any of them so we never found out.

All the well-known towns that were mentioned in the early days of the invasion were all within a few miles of Barneville, such as St. Lo, Caen, Avranches, Coutances, and others. They were very badly shot up and the French were not doing anything about rebuilding. Railroads were not operating, and life in general seemed pretty much at a standstill. There was a general air of apathy and indifference on the part of the French, as though they were waiting for someone from the outside to come to their assistance to get things going again. This attitude probably has changed since de Gaulle has taken over, but I don't know as I haven't been back in France since I left Barneville.

While at Barneville, I made one trip to see Brest. The total destruction of that city, its port facilities and harbor cannot be described. It had to be seen to realize its complete and total waste. The poor people were drifting back to it at the time I visited it, but where they were to live, I don't know—in cellars and caves, I suppose—as they are doing in so many of the destroyed cities, all over Europe. How one man could be responsible for so much destruction and suffering, not only among the conquered nations but among his own people, and escape an assassin's bullet is difficult to understand? The American people wouldn't stand for it, of course; the Germans are, of course, a different breed of cat.

Also, while at Barneville I made one visit to Ninth Army which was then at Maastricht, Holland. I remained several days as they were prepared to jump off on an attack and were waiting for favorable weather so the air could be used. The weather remained bad so I finally returned to Barneville before the attack was launched. It finally came off on November 16, and drove the Krauts across the Roer in most of the Ninth Army sector. It was in this attack that the 102nd had its first offensive fighting, although they had been in a defensive role for a short time prior to that.

Do you remember Reybold who had the 15th Cavalry at Maxey? He just came in to see me. He was wounded and taken prisoner in Normandy, and has been on Guernsey as a PW until released on VE Day. I have the 15th Cavalry, which is now the 15th Cavalry Group, in my corps. Have had them ever since the 1st of February, as a matter of fact, and they have given a very good account of themselves. Reybold is on his way home, as are all released PWs, I believe.

Must close now, darling, Andy

May 22, 1945
Beckum, Germany

My darling:

To continue my progress through France and Europe, in general. While at Barneville I made the trip to Maastricht and returned when we left Barneville for Belgium I spent the night in Paris. So, all told, I spent three nights in Paris, but it was cold and dark at night, so all we did was sleep there. No gay life at all. General officers were put up, free of charge, at The Plaza, and our apartments were very elegant. I had a bedroom, living room, and tremendous bath each time, that, in peace time, would probably have cost a young fortune daily. However, we couldn't enjoy our surroundings because there was no heat in the hotel and the only way to keep warm was to go to bed. NO hot water either. Charlie Brown was with me each time and he, too, had very sumptuous lodgings. We had our first steam heat and hot water after we reached Holland and Belgium.

Our next headquarters were at Tongres, Belgium, where we arrived on November 30. We had a modern school building for our offices and I had a fairly comfortable house, except all the windows were blown out by the explosion of a buzz-bomb which landed about four hundred yards from the house the first day we were there. We remained in Tongres for exactly three weeks, and were glad to leave as every day, except for five days, not less than ten and as high as 26 buzz bombs landed in and around the town. Why we were a target we don't know, but we certainly were, and it wasn't pleasant. Fortunately, we had no

casualties, but several civilians were killed and wounded while we were
there. One bomb hit a row of houses a few blocks from where I lived
just before we left and there wasn't enough left of six houses to build
a decent garage. As I recall only four of the occupants were killed,
although about fifty in the neighborhood were wounded. We also received
a couple of V-2 rockets while there. It was a helpless feeling for you
never knew when they would start coming over. And when you heard
the motor shut-off you would only wait and hope it wouldn't come down
on your particular spot. The V-2's cannot be heard at all—the V-1's,
or buzz bombs, sound like a freight train rushing through the air and
look like a cub airplane.

On the 16th of December, we were to have taken over from a
British corps which was under the Ninth Army, and which was located
just north of Sittard, Holland. We had two divisions actually with us
at Tongres, the 78th and the 75th, and the 106th was under orders
to us. But then the German attack in the Ardennes broke, and our
divisions disappeared overnight.[76] So, we were without a job. Finally, on
the 21st of December the First Army headquarters had to pull back so
we were ordered to Heerlen so the First Army could come into Tongres.
As I said before we weren't sorry to leave Tongres and the buzz bombs.
Heerlen will have to be the subject of a later letter.

Must close and do some work. All my love and kisses to you, my
precious, and to Tudy.

As ever, Always yours, Andy

P.S. Bill Wyche has gone to the VIII Corps to replace Middleton, who,
I understand is going back to the States and back on the retired list.
"Wap" Watson[77] has taken Bill's division. "Wap" had a division early in
the Normandy operations but, for some reason, I don't know about, was
reduced. He has been with the 29th Division and was made assistant
division commander and re-promoted to B.G. last winter. Now he has a
division again. He has made a real comeback. Love, Andy

May 26, 1945
Beckum, Germany

My darling:

So, I'll again take up our travelogue. We arrived in Heerlen on the 22nd of December, and were more or less in a reserve status, though we had no divisions attached. Charlie Brown's artillery helped out the XIII Corps artillery because the latter were then holding such a wide front, as every man who could be spared had been sent to the Ardennes. The first two or three weeks in Heerlen were not too pleasant. We had only a very thin line of troops in front of us, and we anticipated a German attack somewhere on the Ninth Army front daily. Had it come, I don't know what the outcome would have been, although everything had been done in the way of constructing defenses that the limited number of available troops could do. It was a ticklish spot, with the Meuse River at our backs, with only two or three pontoon bridges across it. We didn't know whether we might end up in a German prison camp or not.

The Germans had some long-range guns that used to fire at Heerlen once or twice a day, but fortunately were such poor gunners that they never got a round inside the city limits. The German air was quite a nuisance, and gave us particular attention on Xmas Day and New Year's. One of the dirty devils flew down the street in front of my headquarters at treetop level—I think it was on New Years' Day—and machine-gunned civilians who were just coming out of church next door. In spite of the fact that the street was packed with people—mostly women and children—he fortunately didn't hurt anyone. Promptly on the stroke of twelve on New Year's Eve another devil dropped three bombs right in the heart of town, killing three people and wounding several. All of this type of thing is typical of the German. Heerlen was not a military objective, except for the few troops in it, and any damage he did there would not aid his war effort but certainly endangered the lives of innocent civilians.

I probably had my closest escape in Heerlen, and the irony of that experience was that it was fire from friendly weapons. During one of his almost daily nuisance missions, some German planes came over while we were assembling for lunch. We heard the antiaircraft firing, so like curious schoolboys, we went out on the terrace to see what was going on. While standing there, 50 caliber incendiary bullets started falling all around us. One hit the terrace right at my feet, ricocheted through the window, and came to rest in our dining room. George Barker's pointing to the hole in the enclosed picture. Fortunately for Charles Brown, we did go out for he was sitting with his head directly in line with the hole in the window before we went out.

After about the middle of January, when the Ardennes battle swung in our favor, the tension relaxed and the German air activity also stopped. Shortly after that we started to get our divisions, and finally on February 6 we opened our headquarters at Sittard and became operational. Initially, we had for the defense of our sector the 35th Division, the 15th Cavalry Group, and the British 7th Armored Division. We also had our own 79th Division and 8th Armored Division, but had to keep them in reserve because we were building up for the Roer River crossing and for secrecy purposes, the majority of the divisions then being assigned to the Ninth Army, were being held back so as to try to deceive the Germans regarding the impending attack. They (the Germans) were pretty well aware that the attack was coming, but didn't know just where to look for it. On February 23 we attacked, after having been held back for a couple of weeks by the flooding of the Roer by the Germans, who controlled a series of dams near the headwaters of the Roer, and which they had finally blown sufficiently to cause the river to overflow its banks for about ten days.

Also, while in Heerlen, about the 26th of December, General Simpson called up and said Courtney Hodges had asked if he could borrow me for a few days, or at least until the Ardennes situation could be gotten in hand. The reason was that the commander of the 75th Division, whom I'll not name,[18] wasn't doing so well, and he wanted to use me as division commander until he could recommend someone to take it permanently. I had had the 75th for only about two days, while at Tongres, and I too had been anxious about the commander. So, I reported to Matt Ridgway's corps, but Matt said he wanted to give this chap a chance as he thought he was doing better. However, I remained as a sort of assistant to Matt for about four days, but I could feel that Matt was somewhat embarrassed by my presence, as I was senior to him and also a corps commander. So, I told Matt that I was entirely available to him to use in any capacity, but if he felt the 75th was doing alright and he didn't want me to take it over, I thought I ought to return to my corps. My departure had started rumors that the Cops was being disbanded, morale dropped terribly, and I knew I had to get back to stop that. So, I called Courtney, told him the situation, and he said it would be alright to go back to Heerlen. I told him I could return in half a day if he needed me. So, I got back to Heerlen about the end of the month, and morale jumped back to normal with the assurance that the Corps was not to be disbanded. The commander of the 75th did not last, however, and Ray Porter later took over the division. I have had it back with me from shortly after we crossed the Roer up to the present time, and it has done splendidly under Ray.

Always yours, Andy

To understand the situations described in this letter, reference is made to the official XVI Corps history, which states that although the Seventy-eighth and the 106th infantry divisions had been assigned to the XVI Corps in early December when the XVI Corps Headquarters was in Tongres, Belgium, these divisions were subsequently assigned to the XIX Corps in anticipation of the Roer River crossing operation. Additionally, although the Seventy-fifth was assigned to the XVI Corps on December 9 with the intention of relieving the British XII Corps on December 16, also in preparation for the Roer River crossing operation, all these plans were changed out of necessity by the German Ardennes offensive. As part of the US Army's response to the German Ardennes offensive, the US First Army Headquarters occupied the XVI Corps Headquarters at Tongres, necessitating the XVI Corps move forward to Heerlen, closer to the Ninth Army Headquarters at Maastricht.

General Omar Bradley suggested that the Eighty-second and 101st airborne divisions be turned over to Anderson's XVI Corps under Simpson's Ninth Army. Instead of this command arrangement, General Hodges requested specifically that General Ridgway command the airborne divisions under the XVIII Airborne Corps headquarters and that XVIII Airborne Corps remain under General Hodges' First Army command. Bradley may have wanted a corps headquarters designed more for sustained ground operations like the XVI Corps under Simpson's Ninth Army instead of Ridgway's untested airborne corps headquarters under General Hodges. Regardless, Hodges would not have it and retained XVIII Airborne Corps under his own command.

27 May, 1945
Beckum, Germany

My darling:

Anderson on Reviewing Stand of Sonnelager Displaced Persons Camp, Parade of Russian Nurses, May, 1945.

This afternoon I have accepted an invitation to review the prisoners of war in two of my Russian PW camps. They drill and train as much as they can with no equipment available to them, and are very proud of their accomplishments. After that, I am to attend a concert which is being staged by one of the Russian Displaced Persons Camps in my area. It looks like a very full and busy afternoon. We have about 260,000 displaced persons in our area, of which about 150,000 are Russians, and about 140,000 allied prisoners of war of which about 120,000 are Russians. We have repatriated about 100,000 French, Belgians, Dutch and Russians so far. In other words, we initially had about half a million or more of these people, who had to be gathered up, placed in camps, fed and cared for, hospitalized when necessary and every effort made to make them as comfortable as possible. It has been one of our most difficult problems.

Always yours, Andy

May 29, 1945
Beckum, Germany

My darling:

Am leaving right after lunch today for Maastricht where I shall spend the night. Tomorrow morning there is to be a memorial service at the Ninth Army cemetery at a small town near Maastricht. All corps and division commanders are to attend. It will be the first time I've been west of the Rhine since we moved our headquarters across to the east bank on the 28th of March, to the best of my recollection. Surely a lot of history has been made in those two months. Also, I must say it seems more like two years than two months since I made my first crossing eastward.

As I told you, on Sunday afternoon I went to visit three of my Russian prisoner of war camps. At the first one, the prisoners were all in formation, had dug up some old band instruments and had organized a pretty fair band, and about ten thousand of them had been formed into battalions and passed in review. It was a fine-looking group of men, but what a polyglot mixture—Greeks, Romanians, Armenians, and Chinese, everything imaginable. However, they were very enthusiastic and you would have thought I was Stalin himself. At the next camp, which was not as large, I went through the same thing, with about 5000 passing in review. Here a young Russian girl from a Displaced Persons Camp presented me with a huge bouquet of flowers. I forgot to say that at the first camp, included in the review were a group of Russian female soldiers, who had been used as litter bearers in battle, and perhaps as regular soldiers for all I know. I do know that Russian girls are employed as MPs and in many other jobs in the Russian Army.

At the third camp, they put on what they called a concert. It was pretty corny, although some of the singing wasn't bad, and some of the folk dances were excellent. But heaven knows they tried hard. The camp commander had prepared a "banquet" for my party, consisting mostly of vodka, I believe. However, I had heard about these Russian parties and knew I couldn't contend with our allies in a drinking match. I really did have a good excuse to get back as I had been gone all afternoon. So, when the concert was over I excused myself, much to the disappointment of the Russian officers. They are hospitable people and what little they have they wish to share with you. Also, they appear to be extremely appreciative of our efforts to make them as comfortable as conditions will permit.

Always yours, Andy

June 2, 1945
Beckum, Germany

My darling:

The luncheon with our British friends was very nice and cordial. They turned out a guard of honor for me, which I had to inspect. We then went to General Crocker's quarters, which is a castle belonging to some Austrian princess, who lives somewhere on the place. It was not particularly impressive, either in appearance or furnishings—pretty much down at the heel. However, not bad and the state dining room was really quite nice. It was a very large room and had many windows, whereas the remainder of the place was rather dark and gloomy. We had the Britishers favorite noontime drink, which they call "gin and bitters." Why the "bitters" I don't know as all it consists of is gin and lime juice, bottled lime juice. It isn't bad, however. The meal was very good—hors d'oeuvres, soup, roast lamb and mashed potatoes, carrots, and peas. The dessert was fresh strawberries which were ruined by having been placed in a vile tasting gelatin. At the meal, we had wine. Taisey said the enlisted men's mess was "lousy." But, of course, our soldiers are unquestionably the best fed in the world, and the comparison is unfavorable whenever they eat in the messes of our Allies.

On Wednesday, I have to go to Roermond, Holland, where at 2 o'clock a street is to be named for me—Andersonweg. Weg, I suppose, means street. It is in honor of the XVI Corps and is their method of expressing their appreciation for the liberation of the city by the corps on March 1st. In the meantime, I must prepare an address for delivery on the occasion. I was tactfully informed that it is always customary to mention the Queen and the royal family in any public address, so I've got to work that in somehow. Will tell you more about the ceremony after it is over.

Must close now, precious, and perhaps start on that address.

Always yours, Andy

Hermann Goering Strasse Becomes Anderson Avenue, 1945.

To this day, the people of Roermond celebrate their liberation from the Germans with a parade every March 1.

Major General Anderson with Burgomaster John Joosten Roermond on June 6, 1945

June 6, 1945
Beckum, Germany

My darling:

Yesterday I went to inspect two Polish displaced persons camps. They are so grateful for what we have done for them, which isn't too much. But at least we have gotten them into decent buildings, are feeding them, and clothing them as best we can. The village leader in one of the camps was a Polish major who spoke fairly good English. He has established a school for the children, many of whom have never been to school before, a workshop where the women mend clothes, repair shoes, and make clothes when we can obtain material for them. The stories he told me of how these people were driven by force from their homes into German slavery were many and horrible. It is difficult to believe that barbarism and cruelty of the nature displayed by the Germans could exist in this age of so-called civilization. One little girl, about five years old, was shown me—a pretty little blue-eyed girl, clean and dressed up in her best, which wasn't too good—whose twin sister and mother had been taken away into Germany, but this little girl was overlooked as it hadn't occurred to the Germans that there might be <u>two</u> babies in the bed. However, she was later found and was carried into Germany in charge of another Polish woman. It is not known where the mother and sister are, nor where her father may be. That is just one example of the ruthless, cruel and inhuman treatment visited on innocent people by the beasts who call themselves supermen.

As a technical advisor to the 1929 Geneva Convention, then-Major Anderson was present to advise the US policymakers about the realities of modern warfare. He had experienced the terror of poison gas; as he said in his diary, he "got a whiff or two." He had been into no-man's land, on patrols to capture enemy soldiers for intelligence purposes. He had seen to the care of wounded Germans. The rules adopted in 1929 were intended to minimize the horror and brutality of warfare and to protect combatants and noncombatants from impulsive and capricious acts of retribution and revenge.

So, how troubled now-Major General Anderson must have been with the realities of total war. Total war in 1945 meant the civilian populations of cities were legitimate targets of bombing campaigns from artillery or bombers. Total war in 1945 meant civilians were considered war assets that must be neutralized to achieve victory. The displaced persons' camps were but the tip of the iceberg. The horrors of the slave labor and concentration camps included the use of industrial methods of extermination and disposal of human remains. American soldiers of the 106th captured at the Battle of the Bulge were sent to slave labor camps, not military prisoner of war camps. In these slave labor camps, the Americans experienced the brutality of a system designed to extract as much work for as little food as possible. Some survived to witness for their comrades who had died. These horrors were well-documented and common knowledge by the end of the war.

Total war was a far cry from the gentlemanly rules of war agreed upon in Geneva in 1929. General Anderson's letters to his wife give but a small glimpse of the effect that total war with widespread death and destruction had on him.

June 6, 1945   Sennelager Displaced Persons Camp, Germany

My darling:

Polish Book Marks from Coin and Button and Scrap Cloth, presented to General Anderson, June 1945.

Poor as the major was, when I left he presented me with two books as a token of his appreciation and that of his people for what we have done for them. The books were "Poland between Two Wars" and the other is the story of the Polish air squadron which has worked with the British and which has made a splendid record for itself in this war. The Poles are intensely proud of it.

In each book was a marker in the Polish colors, red and white, and on each marker a metal Polish eagle. The eagles apparently had been filed by hand out of a coin or uniform button or ornament of some kind. When I have read the books, I'll send them to you, with the markers.

As I walked into the school, all the little children were lined up on each side of the entrance walk. First, a little tot about four handed me a bouquet of flowers, after much prompting by one of the teachers. Then as I walked up the walk, the little children along each side threw flowers along my path, and greeted me in Polish. I felt a little foolish, but I know these people are truly grateful for their liberation, and keep referring to us constantly as their liberators and benefactors. Poor people! How I pity them and what sufferings they have undergone. At the second camp the children presented flowers to me—about sixty youngsters—and the bouquets ranged from four or five flowers up to enormous collections. There were with me, besides Mac, three other officers and they all had their arms full of flowers. They filled the back of a jeep.

The enclosed picture was brought to me by a Russian office yesterday. It was taken the day I visited the Russian prisoner of war camp, and is the occasion I told you about in a previous letter. The Russian girl handing me the flowers came from a neighboring Russian displaced persons camp. The Russians too appear to be very grateful for what we have been able to do for them in the bettering of their living conditions.

Always yours, Andy

June 12, 1945
Brussels, Holland, and Chantilly, France,

My darling:

I spent Sunday night in Brussels, but didn't do anything except sleep there. Had a very swanky suite at the Astoria Hotel. The city was full of British as that is their principal leave center on the continent. It is supposed to be a very gay city, but I didn't see any of the night life. The peace did seem to be more nearly normal than any city I have been in on the continent. Yesterday we continued the trip and arrived at this place, Chantilly, at about two in the afternoon. Our headquarters are in the building of the Rothschild estate, and are surrounded by beautiful grounds and a young forest preserve. Herman Goering had his headquarters here during the occupation of France. Charlie Brown and I have another much smaller estate for our quarters. It is about two miles outside town and is also surrounded by beautifully kept formal gardens, but on a much smaller scale. It used to belong to a rich Brazilian but I don't know who the present owner is. It contains six tremendous bedrooms, three baths, also of tremendous size, and library, living room, parlor, dining room and kitchen arrangements, of course. Servants quarters are in the lodge at the gate and over a four-car garage. Will have a picture taken of it when I get a chance, and send it to you. But I'd give it all for a one room shack with you. The furnishings are unusually ornate which is probably due to the South American influence of the former owner.

Love, Andy

July 10, 1945
Auxerre and Marseilles, France

Darling:

Am mailing you the photo album, sent to me by the Russian colonel who commanded the PW camp where the PWs erected the monument to their many dead; the two books presented me by the commander of a Polish displaced persons camp, including the book markers in each book that I described to you at the time the books were given me; the medal of honor of the City of Roermond, presented to me on the day of the street dedication ceremonies, and, finally, a little folder of pictures of our various command posts in Germany.

There is also included in the package an automobile flag made by Russian PWs and presented to me, which they insisted I fly on my car when I visited their camps. It so happened I didn't visit any camps after the presentation, so I didn't have to injure anyone's feelings. Apparently, it was handmade from such materials as they could pick up.

All my love, darling, Andy

July 15, 1945
Cannes, France

My darling:

It is really hot down here, and I would enjoy that part of this visit if I were properly dressed for it. But wool clothing is a bit too much for real enjoyment of hot weather.

This morning we made a tour of Cannes bay in a speed boat, which is at my disposal. It was very nice and cool, and the water is beautiful. So clear and blue, and, throughout the whole bay, you can see the sandy, white bottom regardless of the depth of the water. But I still cannot get any real pleasure out of this without you and Tudy. Also, I can assure you that despite the beauty of the place, I never want to come back after I get back home. We have everything, and more, than they can give us over here.

Bob Hope and his entertainment group are spending the weekend here in the same hotel that we are in. Last evening, he came up and introduced himself to me and then brought up Colonna and introduced him to me. He [Hope] is an extremely attractive individual and apparently unspoiled by his success. I talked to him for ten or fifteen minutes, and found him to be genuinely interested in affording amusement for the soldiers, and no indication that he is seeking publicity for himself. As I told you, in a letter from Marseille, he was entertaining in that area while I was there, but I didn't see him then. He next goes to Bremen to entertain the 29th Division, which is occupying that place.

Bob Hope and Jerry Colonna with Band Members, Entertained by Officers of the 102nd, Cannes, France, July 1945.

In reading the above paragraph over, I find I failed to describe Colonna who is a nice chap too—quite young and with the most flowing mustache you ever saw, except Boy Lee's. I told him I was quite ashamed of my puny effort after viewing his. I didn't meet any of the feminine members of the group, of which there appeared to be about a half dozen. I suppose he didn't introduce them because they feared I would take them away from them. As a matter of fact, they were a rather scrubby looking lot, and I'm not sure they were members of his troupe, but may have been French friends, or at least some of them.

It is hot as the devil in my room so I'm going to close, darling, and go outside. Please write often. All my love and kisses to you, my precious, and to Tudy.

As ever, Always yours, Andy

July 16, 1945
Cannes, France

My darling:

Yesterday afternoon "Sparky" Lang and Faulkner of the artillery, and Gatlin of the 406th Infantry, all of the 102d, of course, blew in, and I've been hearing all about the 102d ever since. And very pleasant and interesting accounts, although they have been a little foggy as to details, as all three have been celebrating their arrival. Busbee is temporarily in command, much to their delight, but Keating is due back next week, which does not meet their pleasure. They all agreed that Pat Fox has been the real spark plug of the division, and they said everyone—officer and soldier alike—grieved the day he left the division. The new assistant division commander is a cavalryman, Colonel Biddle, of whom I have heard, but I know little about him.

Last night Charles, Mac and I had just about finished dinner when the above three arrived and joined us at our table. Before they had finished dallying with their food—they were more interested in liquid refreshments—Bob Hope and his group of about 12 or 15 people arrived and occupied an adjoining table. The fun started then. First thing I knew "Sparky" was playing the harmonica, and he also had a pair of castanets. Harry Faulkner and Sparky were singing some Russian song they had picked up, and in spite of their condition, gave a creditable performance. They received a big hand from Bob Hope's party. "Sparky" announced that he had never expected to entertain Bob Hope. At any rate, the 102d Division song had to be rendered tear jerkingly as well as humorously. By this time Bob Hope and Colonna got into action, and from then until 10:30, about an hour and a half, I laughed until my head ached and the tears ran down my cheeks. It really was an entertaining evening, and I must say, some of the best humor came from Sparky's and Harry's antics. I don't know whether you remember Faulkner or not. He is from Georgia and a typical fun-loving country boy. He is very clever, as is Sparky. They didn't make fools of themselves in the slightest degree, although I was afraid they would when they first embarked on their effort to entertain Bob Hope and his crowd. It turned out very well, and I, for one, was highly entertained.

And, darling, write often for I need your letters so much. I'm really pretty lonely, but, at that, it's better than being indefinitely in the Pacific, as so many are. All my love and kisses to you, my precious, and to Tudy.

As ever, Always yours, Andy

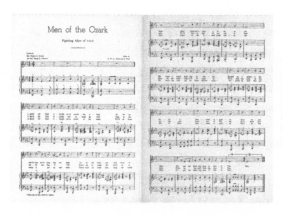

'Men of the Ozarks' Performed by 'Sparky' Lang, Faulkner of the Artillery, and Gatlin of the 406th, July 1945.

This letter is the last one from General Anderson's time overseas. In one of his last official acts, on August 2, 1945, he presented the Bronze Star medal to his aide, Captain Guy R. McFall of Pickens, South Carolina, for meritorious service in connection with military operations against the enemy from February 23, 1945, to May 9, 1945.

On August 11, 1945, Anderson joined a fatigued group of general officers who returned to the United States.

General Anderson's active military service in World War II was over. His military accomplishments were soon to be recognized officially. It was a time to begin to reflect on a life of service, sacrifice, and accomplishment.

CHAPTER 13

AFTER THE WAR

1945-1976

After General Anderson's return to Washington in August 1945, he needed time to adjust to civilian life. From the frontlines in Europe, where death and deprivation were everywhere, to a world at peace in a city without a care, the sudden emergence into a comfortable world of family must have been startling, disorienting, and painful.

Anderson's head must have spun to substitute the tree-lined avenues of Washington with its honking cars, full restaurants, and well-dressed people for the damage he had just witnessed and of which he had been a part. Artillery barrages, casualty reports, and the constant anxiety of the unknown were gone. Gone were the prisoner of war camps, the displaced persons camps, and the slave labor concentration and extermination camps. No longer did he have to look upon every person as either friend or foe.

He was admitted to a hospital to treat newly diagnosed glaucoma. Although he had never complained of any vision problems in Europe, the high pressure in his eyes seriously threatened his sight. Fortunately, the use of pilocarpine eye drops controlled the problem, and he maintained his ability to see. He went before a formal medical board, a formal review of the fitness of the service member. While the proceedings can be anxiety-provoking and even humiliating for the service member, for Anderson they were formal, respectful, and timely.

The board found that his glaucoma condition was severe, but treatable. He was granted a partial disability and found unfit for continued active military service. Within months, that finding was reversed, and he was declared fit for inclusion in the "active" list of retired general officers. As a general officer on the active retired list, Anderson remained on active duty serving on the Incentive Pay Board, until his retirement in June 1946.

The end of Anderson's military career contrasts with those of his fellow Ninth Army corps commanders. The XIII Corps Commanding General Alvan Gillem, promoted to lieutenant general in June 1945, remained on active duty and was asked in October 1945 to chair the Board for Utilization of Negro Manpower, a group of politicians and general officers convened to examine the segregation policies of the Army. The XIX Corps Commanding General Raymond McLain, promoted to lieutenant general in September 1945, remained on active duty and stayed in Germany as commanding general of the XIX Corps. He later became comptroller of the Army and served on President Eisenhower's National Security Training Commission.

In the autumn of 1945, Eisenhower was appointed Army Chief of Staff, succeeding his friend and mentor General George C. Marshall. Army Chief of Staff is the highest-ranking position in the US Army. This person is responsible for all the activities of the service. It is a position of great responsibility and authority. Although the main effort of the Army Chief of Staff in the post-war years was demobilization of the wartime service, many challenges remained, including the occupation of Germany and Japan. The containment of Josef Stalin and the Soviets, with their ambitions to expand their influence in Europe, became an increasingly difficult priority of the President Truman administration. There were many other tasks at hand: the desegregation of the Army, the reconstruction of Europe, the reorganization of the Army, and the creation of the United States Air Force from the Army Air Corps. These challenges were all complicated, difficult questions of policy and protocol.

In the autumn of 1945, Anderson received official recognition for his efforts in World War II. He was awarded the Distinguished Service Medal and the Legion of Merit.

Anderson Receiving Distinguished Service Medal from General Simpson. In Attendance, left to right, were Mrs. Ruth Simpson, Mrs. Sue Anderson, and Miss 'Tudy' Anderson, Washington DC, November 1945.

THE CITATION FOR THE DISTINGUISHED SERVICE MEDAL

Major General John B. Anderson rendered distinguished services from September 1944 to February 1945 and from 9 March to 8 May 1945 as Commanding General of the XVI Corps. Shortly after his arrival in Normandy, his command, together with Headquarters III Corps, was given the task of processing, supplying and equipping for combat Ninth Army units arriving on the continent. Assuming sole responsibility for this mission in November 1944, he overcame great difficulties of distance and lack of facilities. At the same time, he was made responsible, within the area occupied by his command, for the security of the west coast of the Normandy peninsula and for the smooth and prompt movement of supplies from staging to combat areas. In the Ardennes campaign, he and members of his staff rendered important assistance to the Commanding General, XVIII Airborne Corps, in formulating plans for crushing the German onslaught. After the successful conclusion of the Roer River offensive, he organized and massed troops and equipment. He made the plans for and directed the assault which secured a bridgehead across the Rhine River for the Ninth Army. His command participated in the reduction of the Ruhr pocket, and then established military government in a six-thousand-seven-hundred-square-mile area encompassing the Ruhr district. He displayed exceptional ability in planning and directing combat operations, accomplishing great successes with a minimum loss of life. By his resolute manner, sound decisions and wealth of professional knowledge, General Anderson inspired the respect, confidence and loyalty of his subordinates and contributed substantially to the successful operations of the United States Army in Europe.

THE CITATION FOR THE LEGION OF MERIT

Major General John B. Anderson (Army Serial No 03686), United States Army, for exceptionally meritorious conduct in the performance of outstanding services, as Commanding General, XVI Corps, from 9 May 1945 to 10 June 1945. During this period, Major General Anderson was responsible for the establishment of military government in an area of over 4,5000,000 population. In addition, he was responsible for the care, feeding, hospitalization and administration of over 600,000 Allied prisoners of war and displaced persons uncovered by the Corps during its combat operations, and repatriation of nearly 200,000 of these personnel. This mission was successfully accomplished, and law and order were maintained through the outstanding leadership of Major General Anderson. Entered military service from Iowa.

The Distinguished Service Medal is awarded to individuals who have distinguished themselves by exceptionally meritorious service in a position of great responsibility. It is fourth in precedence after the Congressional Medal of Honor, the Distinguished Service Cross, and the Silver Star Medal.

Anderson frequently wore his Legion of Merit medal, with its solid enameled magenta bar, on the left lapel of his civilian jackets, which made a lasting impression on his grandchildren.[79] The Legion of Merit was usually only given to senior officers; in the Army, the medal could be authorized by a lieutenant general, 0-9, to be given "for meritorious conduct in the performance of outstanding services and achievements." Most corps and many division commanding officers in good standing at the end of World War II received this decoration. From 1942-1944, it was awarded frequently for a wide variety of achievements. With the creation of the Bronze Star

Medal in 1944, the Legion of Merit was reserved for more notable achievements. The Legion of Merit is sixth in order of precedence of all US military decorations.

The task of writing the official history of World War II began in the autumn of 1945. Numerous organizations and individuals, from the highest-ranking politicians and generals to lower-ranking officers and the enlisted, began to document their accounts of the war. General Eisenhower wrote his *Report by the Supreme Commander to the Combined Chiefs of Staff on the Operations in Europe of the Allied Expeditionary Force*. General Jacob L. Devers wrote *Report of Activities, Army Ground Forces, World War II*. General Anderson contributed to the Army-Navy journal publication *United States at War*. Detailed and comprehensive, these accounts look back on the events of the war from a strategic and tactical point of view. Of necessity, these publications lack many human elements that letters and contemporaneous writings contain.

The XVI Corps was officially inactivated on December 7, 1945, at Camp Kilmer, New Jersey. *The History of the Sixteenth Corps from its Activation to the End of the War in Europe* was written and published by Infantry Journal Press, Washington, in February 1947. It is a slim volume with colorful unit insignia and maps. The photos are black and white, interspersed throughout the large format pages.

With the official histories of the XVI Corps came the unofficial ones, including the following from Sergeant McPherson Gaines of Warrenton, Virginia. The cover letter address to General Anderson describes the *Wild Tales from Midnight Chow*, written by one of the enlisted men in the headquarters kitchen company, as a series of vignettes about the everyday life of the enlisted man of the XVI during his time in France, Belgium, and Germany. The personal account of the corps' history must have warmed General Anderson's heart; he kept the simple, stapled document all these years.

December 22, 1946 Charlottesville, Virginia

My dear General Anderson,

Although the history of our XVI Corps has already been written, there is a side which does not include the purely military. In an attempt to summarize a few of the "bull sessions" and "extra-curricular activities" of the enlisted staff of G-3, the enclosed has been drafted. Originally, I had intended it only for "Sgt. Hamilton's boys," but you were visiting us so often, we felt you were a member of our little family circle. The fact that you entered and did not demand we "snap to" if we were working drew a great deal of respect, and your "good morning" never failed to win our appreciation.

It has not been my intent to stick strictly to facts. The actual vocabulary used would have, in many instances, failed to pass the standards of the Hayes Office,[80] so it had to be temporized. In some cases, new stories were added; in others, the incident written about had to be deleted from or added to. From this "melting pot" Wild Tales from Midnight Chow has come forth.

McPherson W. Gaines,
University of Virginia School of Law

Preface

"*The following incidents are compiled purely from the memory of a member of the XVI Corps. They represent the carrying out of a promise made to a friend during a midnight meal along the Holland-German border early in 1945. It is respectfully dedicated to one Sgt. Vernon W. Hurlbut, whose story-telling prowess far excels that of the writer, but who exacted a promise to write down some of the thoughts and stories that were swapped in the wee-sma' [81]one during that memorable winter of 1944-45.*

"*A war-time ocean voyage was completed! The 'Queen Mary' had sailed into the harbor at Gourook, Scotland, with its prize package— Winston Churchill—aboard. Also, aboard were the men of the XVI Corps, and several infantry divisions. The speaker system of the proud queen of the seas emitted war news. The news of the latest German defeat was good, but the thoughts of the boys were not entirely on what the miracles of modern radio brought to them.*

"The night was clear and still, a bit chilly. The stars were bright, like crystals on a blue background in a jeweler's. The north star, that God-made compass of the mariner, belonged in Europe also. The lights in the dwellings ashore began to go out—fisher folk retire early. Untouched by war, these homes of the Scots, among their hills, reminded these war-time travelers of home.

"It did not last long, though. That modern miracle of radio began to bark orders to the men as to know they would de bark the following morning. Then, Churchill gave them a few words, their general talked to them; all went below for bunk fatigue . . .

"The train trip to Southampton followed. Seated in an English-style coach, they stowed their gear. The Red Cross, British personnel, gave them coffee and tarts. Now, English coffee is likened to muddy water; and a tart is good if it is FRESH—but, since it is what we would call a sort of pork with pastry built around it, they do not keep well. Yet, knowing what these people had had to give up in the way of meats, it meant a lot . . .

"After crossing the English Channel on 'The Guernsey,' the men boarded trucks for a trip through Cherbourg on their way to Barneville. A 25-mile journey took them through Cherbourg, one of the ports that had been hard hit by shelling from us and from the enemy, and by both the 8th Air Force and the Luftwaffe. As wheels rolled them southward, native peasants trudged along the road with water buckets; or sometimes they had wine jugs with baskets tightly woven and fitted around them. A few of them tried to sell their wine, but the convoy kept going. Other French would be seen wending their weary path toward the homes they may have left when Hitler's legions had first shoved them out. Travelling in any conveyance they could have acquired, from a one-cylinder auto to a donkey cart, more often walking, these people were struggling to what might still be a dwelling, or maybe reduced to rubble . . .

"Thanksgiving Day the men went to church to thank Him for all He had given them, for what they had at home, and to ask His protection in whatever was to come later. They had turkey. Yes, turkey with all the trimmings; that is all save being home. The wind did not blow too hard that day, and the sand did not get into their food in

too great quantities. It did not rain but 2 hours out of the day, so they had those causes to be thankful also.

"'Whatcha' doin', Wally?'

"'Writin' my wife right now. Got a bar of chocolate here, and some cocoa is cooking on the stove.'

"'Cocoa? What's the reason for celebratin'?'

"'My anniversary. Gotta' bust loose somehow!'...

"About this time, the XVI Headquarters unit moved up to the front. Again the 6-bys rolled and hummed through the small French villages. When asking about the numerous corner buildings missing in the narrow, winding streets, they were told that when the red-ballers did not knock them over, the engineers had to do so for them. These knights of the open road had been chosen for their devil-may-care attitude towards anything and everything to haul vitally-needed supplies to the front. France had little or no rolling stock, and fewer rails left, and it took 'truck cowboys' to shuttle gasoline, food, ammunition to the dogface; it was sorely needed by the consignee, and nothing was to hold up the convoys...

"'Where's the driver of that 4th truck in the 1st serial of the convoy?'

"'Still in the cab of his vehicle, Captain. I'll get him.'

"'Soldier, why didn't you get out as fast as the other drivers?'

"'Well, Sir, I ain't never wore shoes before I got in the Army. Anyway, I just have to drive without them things. Down in Kentucky whare I come from, we don't use no shoes.'[82]

"And so go the problems of a Company Commander...

"The XVI Corps had arrived at the front. The same Kentuckian who seemed to hate using footgear so much gave forth with the songs of his native state that night, and every night until he returned to his own artillery outfit back in France. A good, strong voice, and that old mountain music helped to cheer the boys there in the land of the Belgians...

"Then came the Battle of the Bulge. Evidently, the mad Prussian, Von Runstedt, had thought the men to have too gay a time. War was a bitter business to him, so on 16 December 1944, he decided to change the well-ordered front line painted on the maps at headquarters. Headquarters' became the front line in many cases, so it was decreed that the men of the Corps numbered XVI should get the ___ out of

there, and move in the Land of the Netherlands. A few too many beers made travelling a bit difficult for certain ones, but they managed to make the move on last minute notice—FAST . . .

"The quaint little town of Heerlen, Holland, down in the boot of that country, was the next destination . . . There was a girl there who fixed her blond tresses like Veronica Lake and drew charcoal sketches—and rough sketches they were, but she was quite a looker. Also, there was a pair of children, aged about 10 each, in a brother and sister act with accordions; they could swing a mean set of notes, or play Beethoven, Bach, equally as well. When one received a hankie, and the other a harmonica, their very hearts were thankful. Christmas to them meant giving, without thought of receiving, and although what their mouths said did not penetrate to the G.I. who presented them, their eyes told a wonderful story . . .

"Christmas day found the men in church. A Dutch Reform Church had been loaned to them as a chapel, and 3 padres held services there for the men of all faiths. The Heerlen residents sang 'Silent Night' first in English, and then in their own tongue; they also sang 'O Come All Ye Faithful' the same way to the warriors from across the sea. Men came in battle dress, complete to weapons. A shave and wash made their faces clean, and the service made their souls feel clean. When one of the 3 chaplains went to the pulpit, which was in the center of the south end of the church, up above his congregation, one could see the deep spiritual feeling in each and every face. These men had been allowed to live this long; and they prayed that their God would let them see the end of hostilities to return to the loved ones ever in their hearts. 'Nearer My God to Thee' is not a Christmas hymn; but it certainly was the true feeling of those fellows fortunate enough to be either stationed in the town or on pass to the rest camp . . .

"In January, a notable event occurred. A few tickets became available for the 'Barretts of Wimpole Street', in which Katy Cornell and Brian Aherne were costarring in the ETO. There was the lucky individual who fell heir to one, through the system of drawing names from a hat—one of three tickets designated for the 2,300 men in Corps and its attached troops.

"On his way to the performance, he helped a lady in distress. She had fallen on the ice. In perfect English, she informed him that she was going to the theater. Now, perfect English was not an uncommon thing

in the Netherlands, so it roused nothing in his brain; and since he was going in that direction, he would assist the fair lady. Upon arrival at the entrance to this theater, he explained that it was impossible for him to take anyone but American military personnel into the play; that it was a performance for them alone. The reply was: 'I am afraid there would be no show if I did not go in. You see, I am Katherine Cornell'.....

"Other notables visited the area. 'The Lady with the Million Dollar Legs' was in the Ninth Army area. She visited the Special Service Office of the XVI, where she met that identical man who had befriended Cornell and met Aherne. Marlene Dietrich remembered this man almost a year later, when they chanced to meet in Paris. In her whole time touring the ETO, she had only to roll up the heavy GI winter underwear she wore as far as her knee, and howls of delight would emanate from her soldier audience.

"Soon, the men of the XVI Corps moved into the front line facing Germany. Before this the men had hated to leave newfound friends, but they had been able to look forward to meeting still more. There was no such brightness in the horizon, for now they were moving into the land of the mad paper hanger—where all sang 'Deutschland Uber Alles,' whether behind your back in occupied territory, or in a desperate attempt to bolster their own morale back of the German lines . . .

"Three days later, a bright, sunny day dawned. Time to move again! Everything was packed accordingly, including the gin belonging to certain of the officers. Not all of the gin arrived successfully, though the empty bottles did get there . . .

"Recklinghausen found the operations boys[83] quartered in a one-time Nazi hospital. One end of it contained many potato-masher grenades that had been left there; for Jerry had even used his hospitals as strongholds, under the protection of the Geneva Cross . . .

"En route back from a leave in Paris, a friend of a friend of a friend told these good people of the old XVI, battle-scarred from the ETO, was going home—en route to the Pacific. Well, Pacific or no Pacific, it sounded good—the word home, and the thought that they would be there in a month or so. What matter if it was TWO months, just so they got there! . . .

"But we know that the XVI Corps did not go home for transfer to duty in the Pacific. Elements of the XVI Corps stayed in occupied

*Germany; others did go home for good. In the fall of '45, the old XVI
began to break up. She was Category IV, and could only take high-
pointers with her.*[84] *Thus, many were left behind, and farmed out to
various other units. Some went to Paris, some back to Germany. While
all this was going on, VJ-Day came, amid wild celebrations and the
earnest prayers for peace of all the world . . . The men carried the
following prayer for peace; entitled 'A Soldier's Prayer in Victory.'*

> *"Wait, God, don't go! Though enemies are vanquished*
> > *and blessed Peace has stilled the battle's roar,*
> > *our hearts are seared. A world lies ill and anguished*
> > *with wounds of hate from unrestricted war.*
> *Stand closer. Guide the leaders of our nation.*
> > *make clear their greatest task—their sacred trust—*
> > *to build eternal Peace through toleration*
> > *and lead the world from selfishness and lust.*
> *Grant deeper strength than fury-driven bravery—*
> > *the strength of firm conviction in the right*
> > *of Man to live beyond the fear of slavery*
> > *impressed by force of military might.*
> > *our hands and minds are trained for grim destruction.*
> > *now guide our skills to work with greater care*
> > *for lasting Peace and human reconstruction,*
> > *this, God, is every thoughtful soldier's prayer.*
> *From distant graves the legions of our martyred*
> > *join hands with countless wounded wracked in pain,*
> > *to beg that dreams they fought for not be bartered*
> > *and sacrificed for economic gain.*
> > *Great God of Wrath, in deep appreciation*
> > *we kneel to bless Your name for battles won.*
> > *Great God of Peace, in earnest supplication*
> > *we ask your help until Your will be done.*

*"The rest of the fall, and the winter months, dragged very, very
slowly by, until most of us got home. It is needless to express the
happiness of each and every one at returning to his native shore.
Europe has its points, but she is out-pointed by the USA. And these
little tales told at the midnight chow table, along with many others,*

will stand in their memories for the years to come."

As evidenced by the quality of the writing, it is no surprise that McPherson Gaines pursued a legal career.

General Anderson received news on May 14, 1946, that the Netherlands government had awarded him the Order of Orange-Nassau, degree of Grand Officer, with the Swords, effective September 25, 1945. Throughout the remainder of his life, he displayed this award in the honor position in his living room in Washington, DC. The prominent place for this honor reflects his appreciation of the Netherlands government. With this decoration, and the parade given Anderson by the people of Roermond, the Netherlands honored him beyond any recognition received by official action of the United States government. There are six classes to the Order of the Orange-Nassau; the degree of Grand Officer is second highest. The eight-pointed Maltese cross decoration may be worn on a necklet or on the left chest. Swords denote military service; during and after World War II, the award was bestowed upon both members of the Netherland's military and foreign military members who helped liberate the Netherlands from Nazi occupation. The Order of the Orange-Nassau ranks with the Order of the British Empire in the United Kingdom.

Order of the Orange-Nassau, Grand Officer, with Swords. Presented to Anderson by the Netherlands Government, May 1946.

Another foreign government award was La Croix de Guerre 1940 avec Palme, awarded Anderson on August 29, 1947, by the Belgium government "for exceptional military services in the liberation of Belgium and in its defense 1944-1945." The bronze medal is a Maltese cross with eight points and crossed swords suspended by a red-striped ribbon. The Belgium fouragere of 1940 is three twisted cords of silk (for officers) in red and green ending in a knot with a metal tag and was an award to members of a military unit cited twice or more. The Belgium Croix de Guerre 1940 award was given primarily for bravery or other military virtue on the battlefield. Other notable US Army recipients were Patton, Montgomery, and General Carl Spaatz.

Smilin Jack

Anderson soon had another task to occupy his days. Tudy was to marry. She met Harper Elliott Van Ness Jr., at a Christmas party in December 1946, at the home of her friend "Liz" Eisinger, from her days at Mount Vernon Seminary School. Harper was nicknamed "Jack," after an incident his plebe year at the US Naval Academy. Under the watchful eye of an upperclassman at a table of fellow plebes, Harper caught the upperclassman's attention. "What are you smiling at, Smilin' Jack?" he demanded. "Smilin' Jack" was a well-known comic book figure of the day, a rogue with the ladies and a swashbuckling pilot. As one of the gentler initiation customs of the military service, the giving of nicknames, some flattering and others not, was part of the bonding process of cadets and midshipmen. I expect "Smilin' Jack" Van Ness was happy to adopt the nickname. He kept it all his life.

Jack Van Ness

Smilin' Jack was a drop-dead gorgeous, glamorous carrier pilot who had caught Tudy's eye. Stanley Matthews, the West Point cadet and decorated officer who had figured so prominently in Anderson's and Tudy's letters, was inexplicably no longer "the one" for Tudy. Although not a graduate of West Point, Smilin' Jack's accomplishments and service likely satisfied Anderson. If his daughter would not marry an Army man, a Navy man would have to do.

At the time, Tudy's frame of mind was more complicated. Years later, she explained that she was very unhappy at home. Her father was drinking too much, petulant, and highly critical of her appearance and behavior. As a soon-to-be college graduate, Anderson felt "she should have been doing more" for herself, not just socializing and wasting her time at the Chevy Chase Club. His heroic behavior on the battlefields of Europe was devolving into something meaner at home. Maybe her choice of a Navy man was part rebellion against his temper and behavior?

If Anderson were accepting of his daughter's choice of a Navy man, Mrs. Anderson was not pleased with Tudy's groom-to-be. Her criticism was likely less that he was a Navy man than the fact that he was not from "the right kind of people." Harper "Smilin' Jack" was raised an orphan. His mother died in the autumn of 1919, just three months after his birth. His father left him to be raised by his paternal grandmother and aunts. The family was poor and needed to take in boarders—twenty-five cents a night—to help make ends meet.

Smilin' Jack's life and upbringing were not like Tudy's or Mrs. Anderson's lives. There were no shopping trips to New York City or servants in the kitchen. There was no Judge George Palmer or other father figure to reassure him, to cajole and tease him, or to send him small checks and gifts of Coca-Cola stock. How ironic that Mrs. Anderson, a Southern belle whose own mother was so very conscious and jealous of her social standing; who had married an Army officer from Iowa with little to his name besides his education, his wartime service, and his career ambitions; was now terrified that her daughter was making the same mistake marrying an ambitious man of modest means, Naval Academy education, and honorable wartime service.

Despite these misgivings, the wedding plans proceeded apace. The planning for this event must have rivaled the planning for the Rhine River crossing. The ceremony was to take place at the Washington National Cathedral's St. Mary's Chapel.

General and Mrs. Anderson gathered many of Anderson's West Point classmates and friends for the occasion. The wedding list included West Point Class of 1914 members Clarence Benson, Harrison Brand, Arthur Harris, Paul Paschal, and Xenophon Price. Other West Pointers included Major General and Mrs. James Lester. From his service along the Texas-Mexico border in 1914-1917, Anderson invited General and Mrs. George Eberle and Major General and Mrs. Jonathon W. Anderson. From the time of his service in the Philippines in 1925-1927, he invited Colonel and Mrs. Don Blackburn and General Frederick von H. Kimble. There were several invitees from his time as an instructor at the Army's Command and General Staff College at Fort Leavenworth, including fellow instructor Lieutenant General and Mrs. Manton Eddy and their mutual student General and Mrs. Loyal Haynes. From the

102nd Infantry Division days, there was Colonel and Mrs. George Keyser, chief of staff, and Colonel and Mrs. Sydney Perell, the judge advocate general. And of course, a large contingent from the XVI Corps, including Colonel and Mrs. John Wheeler, Colonel and Mrs. O. McDaniel, Chaplain and Mrs. H. Kellogg, Surgeon Colonel and Mrs. H. Furlong. The wedding had the air of a reunion as well as the celebration of Anderson's daughter's marriage.

Sue Anderson Escorted by Her Father, 1947

As Anderson escorted the bride down the aisle to strains of Handel's "Largo" and Bach's "Air for G String," the double-ring ceremony began.

It had all the majesty and weight of a Roman triumph. Surrounded by friends and family, amidst the crowd of comrades in arms with whom Anderson had spent harrowing days leading men in combat, with majestic music soaring amongst the gothic arches within the confines of the stately Washington National Cathedral, the march down the aisle was another moment that justified all the years of study, of self-denial and self-sacrifice, of hard times and harder self-discipline, and of the personal risks taken in an Army career. General Anderson separated from his Iowa family early in life to pursue a life in the Army. While away at West Point, his mother had died. While away on the Texas-Mexico border, his father died. While heading to the trenches of France, his first marriage failed and ended in divorce. After his service with the Army in World War I, he returned for a brief visit to Iowa in 1918, never to return again. The Army became his family. He served honorably and well, both at home and abroad. He was recognized and rewarded officially. Now, he was rewarded by the gathering of family, friends, and comrades.

With his beautiful daughter on his arm, Anderson had to be so proud. The smiles of his West Point classmates warmed his heart. His sense of decorum likely suppressed the tears that could have easily flowed. Although his heart was full, it would not do to show emotion. He had been through so much with these men—trials of death and destruction, of wastage and horror; in Europe in both wars, he had had to harden his heart and repress any expression of sadness or fear.

These men too had seen and endured many horrors beyond ready understanding. They would understand the general's stoic expression. They would understand his quiet satisfaction at this important moment. The only missing element of his triumphant march down the aisle on the arm of his daughter at the moment of her departure from his sphere was the slave that in a Roman triumph whispered in the conquering hero's ear, "All glory is fleeting."

CHAPTER 14

LEST WE FORGET

While the United States demobilized after World War II, world events rolled on. In the wake of the failure to capture Berlin at the end of the Second World War, the Soviet Union and the Western Allies began an increasingly acrimonious and hostile war for the future of Europe. One aspect of the new "Cold War" was the Soviet Union's decision to deny the Allies land access to Berlin. The city was cut off from all road and train traffic from the west. Supplies of food, fuel, and medicines were cut off.

In response, in June 1948, the Allies began an airlift of essential items for survival. The air forces of the United States, England, France, Canada, Australia, New Zealand, and South Africa flew more than 200,000 cargo flights into the city. As many as 8,500 tons a day were arriving by air, and the Soviets relented. The success of the Berlin Airlift demonstrated the Allies' commitment to containment of the Soviet Union; the Marshall Plan for the economic recovery of Europe likewise reduced significantly the influence of the Soviet Union. The unfinished business of victory required money, patience, and understanding of the long-term needs of the vanquished. Unlike the crushing nature of reparations required by the Treaty of Versailles after World War I, these needs of the vanquished were met by the generosity of the victors.

After the First World War, the United States military let down its guard. Soon after the demobilization of 1919-1920, it recognized a need to train a core cadre of highly competent officers. The Army schools at Fort Sill, Fort Benning, and Fort Leavenworth were the sites of artillery, infantry, and command training.

After World War II, the military also rapidly demobilized but soon recognized threats still existed, especially from the Soviet Union and its proxy states. It sent officers to Army schools as before but also to the best civilian universities like Massachusetts Institute of Technology and Carnegie Mellon to study subjects like nuclear and chemical engineering. For the country's survival, the military needed officers to be highly educated and superbly trained. In particular, nuclear technology, submarine development, advanced aviation, and rocket science dominated the thinking of military planners.

Like Anderson, Smilin' Jack and Tudy moved from service school to service school, having children as they went along. Smilin' Jack attended graduate schools in advanced engineering subjects, earning a master's degree in electrical engineering from the Naval Postgraduate School in Annapolis and an aeronautical engineering master's degree from Rensselaer Polytechnic Institute in Troy, New York.

Anderson became a grandfather three times over. Grandson Elliott Scott was born on September 16, 1948; grandson John Anderson was born on September 8, 1950; and grandson Michael Moore was born on June 6, 1953. Unfortunately, General and Mrs. Anderson were rarely able to spend much time with their grandsons. Tudy was now a Navy wife and, like her mother before her, went where military orders dictated.

General and Mrs. Anderson filled their time with XVI Corps reunions, West Point class reunions, and letters to and from colleagues. Anderson devoted much of his time to keeping alive the memories of his service abroad. After so many years of overseas travel, distance from home, and separation, he longed for the camaraderie of his Army service. While he had been abroad, he dreamed of home and now at home, he held firmly to the relationships formed abroad.

The first XVI Corps reunion took place in Gary, Indiana, and had about 200 attendees. What a thrill it must have been for Anderson to see so many of his old friends! Even some of the wives of old comrades attended; they did not seem to mind the tentlike accommodations nor the rural setting.

In his 1949 Christmas letter to his XVI Corps comrades, he expresses his heartfelt sentiments. They provide a sense of the importance of his service in the XVI Corps and more importantly the value he placed on the memory of those with whom he served.

December 25, 1949   Washington, D.C.

Dear Comrades:

Another year has elapsed since our existence as a military organization ceased. My recollections of those days, when we worked together to bring about the defeat of our enemies, have always been the highlight of my military career. As the years go by, the associations of those days become increasingly dear to me.

During the past year it has been my good fortune to see and visit with a considerable number of Compassites. My fervent wish is that I may eventually renew my acquaintance with everyone who, at any time, served with our Corps. I know that all of you would enjoy, as I do, visiting with your former comrades and recalling the experiences you shared with them during those times of mutual hardships and dangers. To this end, I urge that all former members of the Corps make a real effort to attend our future reunions.

With the opportunity afforded by this, our annual Christmas letter, I wish to express again my appreciation of your loyalty, your devotion to duty, and your contributions to the success achieved by the XVI Corps in World War II. Also, through the medium of this letter, I desire to extend to each of you, and to the members of your families, my sincere wish for a very Merry Christmas and for health, happiness, and prosperity throughout the New Year.

Sincerely,

John B. Anderson
Major General
U.S. Army, Ret.

Anderson, old friends, and family gathered together next in Atlanta, Georgia, in the summer of 1950. Happier and simpler times were recalled and old stories retold.

The XVI Corps was reactivated as an active unit of the US Army in April 1951. It was part of the Far East Command, stationed in Sendai, Japan, supporting the war effort in Korea. No member of the original XVI Corps served in the new outfit. However, it was a source of pride, expressed by Anderson in a newsletter to the original Compassites, that the XVI Corps was active again in the service of the country. It is ironic that in 1951, the XVI Corps headquarters in Japan was established for Japan's protection as opposed to its destruction, as it was planned in 1945.

In February 1952, Anderson had dinner with the ambassador from the Netherlands. From the letter that follows, he seems to have enjoyed recounting the events of early 1945 and the liberation of Roermond and the gratitude expressed directly to him by the people of Roermond.

29 February 1952   Washington, DC

My dear General,

It was a real pleasure meeting you at the Barrister's dinner which I attended at the kind invitation of Mr. Cunningham. I enjoyed hearing about your experiences in Holland and the liberation of Roermond.

It so happens that I have an old history book containing maps of several cities in the Netherlands, among which I also found one of Roermond. It would give me great pleasure if you would accept this map as a remembrance of our meeting and as a token of thankfulness that I and all Dutch people feel for the liberation and the active part you played in it.

With kindest regards, I am
Sincerely yours,
L.R.W. Soutendijk

P.S. The book "Boeken van Geldersse Geschiedenissen" was written by Arend van Slichtenhorst and printed in Arnhem in 1654 by Jacob van Biesen.

Major General & Mrs. Anderson Boston March 1952

Anderson received "The Key to the City" from the Mayor of Boston, the Honorable John B. Hynes, on the occasion of the XVI Corps reunion in 1952. The invitation is another reminder of the esteem in which civilian leaders held veterans of the Second World War.

On August 8, 1952, at the Sheraton Plaza Hotel, Hynes hosted a luncheon honoring Anderson. It was one of the few reunions that Mrs. Anderson attended. The urban setting was more to her liking than canvas tents in the woods.

Anderson and General Simpson exchanged letters in 1952. The two men had definite opinions regarding the role their immediate boss, General Omar Bradley, played in their respective careers. Not only was Bradley's approval needed for command in the European theater of operations, he also controlled all promotions within his Twelfth Army Group. At the end of the war, this group contained four armies: First Army, Third Army, Ninth Army, and the Fifteenth Army. General Patton of the Third Army had been promoted to a four-star rank on April 14, 1945. General Hodges of the First Army had been promoted to a four-star rank on April 15, 1945. Lieutenant General Simpson of the Ninth Army remained a three-star general as did Lieutenant General Leonard Gerow of the Fifteenth Army.

Major General Anderson received the following letter from Lieutenant General Simpson at Christmas, 1952:

15 December 1952   San Antonio, Texas

Dear Andy:

Your letter of 26 November was received and read with great interest. I certainly appreciate you passing this information on to me. I did not know that Bradley had thought so highly of me or that any effort had been made towards my promotion.

Incidentally, Bradley also thought very highly of you. When Millikin was sent from my Army to Geo. Patton's Third Army, Bradley discussed with me what Corps would replace him. He had a list of four Corps commanders in which you were included. I told him I would prefer you to any of the others. Bradley said he agreed with me, that you were his first choice also.

I read where you were detailed as a member of a board to consider incentive pay, I believe it was, and imagine you must have found it interesting work.

For the past year I have had a job as Military Representative of one of the banks here in San Antonio and have been enjoying the work very much. It has given me something to do and has proven both pleasant and interesting. I was called out of town twice to nearby towns since receipt of your letter or would have answered it sooner.

Many thanks, Andy, for telling me of Bradley's nice compliment.

Ruth joins me in sincere regards and best wishes to Sue and you for the Christmas season and for the New Year.

Always,

Sincerely,

Bill

Despite the praise from General Simpson, no promotion was forthcoming for Major General Anderson. The letter of December 1952 gives no hint of the ongoing efforts to secure Simpson the promotion he rated as commanding officer of the Ninth Army.

On July 19, 1954, while J. Lawton Collins was Army Chief of Staff, by special Act of Congress (Public Law 83-508), President Eisenhower approved the promotion of a number of senior officers on the retired list to four-star general. Simpson and Gerow were given their fourth star and promoted on the retired list to full general, the rank appropriate to their last assignment.

In 1954, the movie *White Christmas* was released. It is the fictitious story of a widowed General Waverly who commanded an infantry division in Europe in World War II. After the war, in his retirement, Waverly buys a Vermont country inn and runs it with his daughter and spinster aunt. It is a seasonal business dependent on skiing. The business is not very successful.

Waverly's character is one of a gentle curmudgeon doing his best to run the inn and care for his family. His family treats him with respect. He is courteous to them and dignified in manner. They know how important it is for him to maintain his dignity, especially in the face of mounting financial difficulties. He finds that his dream of running an inn is so different than the business of running an inn. And the business of running an inn, especially one that is failing, is so very different from his success in commanding soldiers.

His friends and family are at a loss as to how to help him. In a poignant scene that speaks to this difficulty, Bing Crosby sings a song that asks the question, "What do you do with a general when he's no longer a general?" It is a universal question that applies not only to General Waverly, but to all generals, officers, and men of the armed services. It is a question Mrs. Anderson and Tudy pondered throughout General Anderson's retirement.

In *White Christmas*, an unfortunate lack of snowfall threatens to end Waverly's dream. In fact, if there is no snow, the upcoming Christmas holiday is going to be the last holiday before financial difficulties force them to close. For audiences of 1954, Waverly's fears must have reminded them of the fears they felt just nine years before during the great German offensive against the American armies at the Battle of the Bulge. And like those American soldiers, General Waverly "soldiers" on, doing his duty and the best he can in the circumstances, even when the circumstances are beyond his control. He is not inclined to ask for nor accept help. He is proud to a fault.

Of course, Bing Crosby steps in. He has a plan to rescue the "old man." Since Waverly is too proud to accept any help, the plan must be carried out in secret. Crosby's character recruits the song and dance team of Rosemary Clooney, Vera-Ellen, and Danny Kaye to fill the inn with the men of Waverly's old command. Crosby goes on national TV and "puts out the word" for a reunion of the "old division" at the general's inn on Christmas Eve. Even though it means leaving their own families on the holiday, out of respect and affection for "the old man," the men of his former division—his "old Army buddies"—happily fill the inn.

In the movie's climatic scene, the general "inspects" the troops. Bugles sound; short speeches are made with words of affection, humor, and respect; and salutes are exchanged. The stage doors are then opened to reveal snow beginning to fall outside.

This story is one about the powers of redemption and resurrection. Waverly's men had repaid his leadership and care of them with their presence and tribute at his time of need. They came to his rescue. Their tribute was a fitting one.

In General Anderson's case, there was no overt need like General Waverly's financial problems, but there was a void in his life after the war. The annual reunion of the XVI Corps and the presence of old Army buddies eased his loneliness and heartache. Over the years, as expected, the number of attendees decreased. Despite that fact, pictures taken at the reunions show both his happy smile and twinkling eyes. The Christmas "Compass Corps" newsletters continued year after year and reveal a true devotion of the men to one another. Like the characters in *White Christmas*, there was true interest and concern for one another among the former military men.

In later years, especially after her father's death in 1976, whenever Tudy saw *White Christmas*, the tears flowed. The movie evokes a strong emotional response from World War II veterans and their families. Tears well up in sympathy and remembrance of General Waverly's devotion to his men and their devotion to him. The poignancy of the message of the movie reminds them of the difficult transition and adjustment to civilian life these veterans endured.

Life went on; events at the White House came and went. On one occasion, General and Mrs. Anderson were invited to attend a dinner. As President of the United States, Eisenhower took the high road and seemingly carried no ill will or hard feelings toward General Anderson.

The issue of promotion of Simpson and other World War II Army commanders was corrected by Presidential Special Order

153.[85] However, no actions were being undertaken to remedy the situation for former corps commanders. This seemed to rankle both Anderson and Simpson. In 1958, in response to a letter from Anderson, Simpson reiterated that he regretted the failure of Anderson to be given the rank commensurate with his service.

San Antonio,   Texas July 10, 1958

Dear Andy:

Your letter of June 30 was received and I was delighted to hear from you again.

A few years ago, I wrote you that during the war I had recommended your promotion to lieutenant general. I would like to repeat what I told you then.

During World War II you commanded the XVI Corps which was one of the three Army Corps permanently assigned to the Ninth Army which was commanded by me. You and the XVI Corps under your command performed in a superior manner during all combat operations which included an attack from the Roer River to the Rhine River, the crossing of the Rhine River, the capture of the Ruhr area, and the encirclement and capture in cooperation with units of the First Army of a pocket of about 350,000 German soldiers.

Because of your splendid record and performance of duty during the entire time you were under my command, I recommended you for promotion to the grade of lieutenant general and I was informed that this recommendation was approved by General Bradley who commanded the XII Army Group of which the Ninth Army was a part.

I have always regretted that you did not receive this promotion which you so richly deserved. I wish to assure you that it was an honor and a pleasure to serve with you and your fine XVI Corps, and I shall always feel most grateful to you for the fine job that you did.

Ruth and I were delighted to have news of you and Sue, and to know that all goes well with you. We are both well. I am Vice President of the Alamo National Bank here and am enjoying the work. We both manage to keep busy.

If we ever come to Washington we shall certainly let you know. If
you ever come through here please let us know. It would be grand to
see you both again. Ruth joins me in sending our warmest regards and
best wishes to you both.

Sincerely,
Bill
William H. Simpson, General, U.S. Army, Retired

In this personal letter attesting to the affection between the two
old soldiers, it seems to me that Simpson is resigned to the fact that
he can do no more to advocate for a promotion for Major General
Anderson.

In October 1961, *Washington Post* columnist Drew Pearson
wrote an article[86] that sheds light on the rising tide of "Monday
morning quarterbacking" of events in 1945. While the article
examines Eisenhower's decision to withdraw US Army forces to the
Elbe and to "leave" Berlin to the Russians, it also gives insight into
his frame of mind as the end of the war drew near, and a possible
explanation for the oversight of Anderson's promotion.

Drew Pearson wrote:

> "*The friends of former President Harry Truman,
> Democrat, are a bit miffed with President Kennedy,
> Democrat, for bowing to former President Dwight D.
> Eisenhower, Republican, over Berlin. They think Mr.
> Kennedy should stick up for his own side a little more.
> "The famous feud between the two former Presidents
> began over Berlin when Mr. Truman, in a speech in
> San Francisco during the 1952 presidential campaign,
> charged that Gen. Eisenhower was responsible for
> leaving Berlin isolated, 110 miles away from West
> Germany, with no guaranteed right of access. Ike has
> not spoken to Harry since.
> "In this feud between two famous former
> Presidents, Mr. Kennedy has appeared to side with Gen.
> Eisenhower. He has sent Gen. Lucius Clay, Ike's close*

friend and former subordinate, back to Berlin, though Clay assumed responsibility in his memoirs for failure to get access rights to Berlin. On top of this, Secretary of State Rusk hastened to apologize to Gen. Eisenhower when the State Department issued a history of Berlin containing the statement that 'the Western armies could have captured Berlin... but the Supreme Commander, Gen. Eisenhower, believed they could be more usefully employed against the major German forces elsewhere. As a result, the Soviets captured Berlin.'

CHURCHILL'S TELEGRAMS

"In contrast to the Kennedy Administration's rush to apologize to General Eisenhower, here is what Winston Churchill had to say when the General diverted American forces away from Berlin in the closing days of the war.

"'If we deliberately leave Berlin to them (the Russians),' Churchill wired Eisenhower direct on March 31, 1945, 'even if it should be in our grasp, the double event may strengthen their conviction, already apparent, that they have done everything. Further, I do not consider myself that Berlin has yet lost its military and certainly not its political significance.'

"Gen. Eisenhower had previously advised Stalin that he proposed to make the main American thrust along the Erfurt-Leipzig-Dresden line, instead of driving on Berlin. He had ordered United States forces when they reached Potsdam, a suburb of Berlin, back to the Elbe.

"Republicans, who criticized the State Department for its implied criticism of Gen. Eisenhower in its 'Berlin Background' pamphlet, claimed that the Big Three had agreed at Yalta to let the Russians take Berlin. Churchill's emphatic telegrams prove just the opposite.

IKE SWITCHED PLAN

"Telegraphing President Roosevelt on April 1, Churchill said he had no desire to lower the prestige of Gen. Eisenhower in his relations with the Russian commanders. But, he continued:

"'All we sought was a little time to consider the far-reaching changes desired by Gen. Eisenhower in the plans that had been concerted by the Combined Chiefs of Staff at Yalta and had received you and my joint approval . . .'

PERSISTENT CHURCHILL

"In his April 1 wire to FDR, Churchill went into considerable detail about Gen. Eisenhower's switch in plans.

" 'Gen. Eisenhower, in his estimate of the enemy's resistance, to which I attach the greatest importance, now wishes to shift the axis somewhat to the southward and strike through Leipzig, even perhaps as far south as Dresden. He withdraws the Ninth U.S. Army from the northern group of armies . . .

"'I say quite frankly that Berlin remains of high strategic importance. Nothing will exert a psychological effect on despair upon all German forces equal to that of the fall of Berlin . . .

"'If they (the Russians) also take Berlin, will not their impression that they have been the overwhelming contributor to our common victory be unduly imprinted in their minds, and may not this lead them into a mood which will raise grave and formidable difficulties in the future? . . .

"'I further consider that from a political standpoint we should march as far east into Germany as possible, and that should Berlin be in our grasp, we should certainly take it.'

"Churchill also sent a telegram to Gen. Eisenhower, March 28, 1945, complaining that the General had sent a telegram direct to Stalin changing military strategy.

"Regarding this Churchill commented: 'We all thought that this went beyond the limits of negotiation with the Soviets by the Supreme Commander in Europe.'

"When the British Prime Minister did not get a satisfactory reply from President Roosevelt, he sent him another telegram, April 5.

"'I still think it was a pity that Eisenhower's telegram was sent to Stalin without anything being said to our Chiefs of Staff or to our Deputy Air Chief Marshall Tedder, or to our Commander-in-Chief Field Marshall Montgomery,' Churchill telegraphed.

"Seven days later, Roosevelt was dead. No one was in a position to reverse Gen. Eisenhower. And that's how the Russians got to Berlin; also, how the Berlin problem, which we are still arguing about, got started."

The politics of the time, the continued arguments about the "surrender" of Berlin to the Russians in 1945 and the implications of that decision, were unsettling. In the autumn of 1961, President Kennedy and his administration was still viewed as young and inexperienced. There was a fascination with espionage. James Bond books and movies captivated the imagination of the president and the populace. Movies like *Doctor Strangelove* and *Seven Days in May* examined the lines of authority of military and political figures. These questions and others were posed. How to contain the Russians, what to do in Vietnam, and what was the proper role of the military in a nuclear world? The United States had barely averted a nuclear confrontation with Russia over nuclear-capable missiles in Cuba during the Cuban Missile Crisis of October 1960, and the Vietnam War was pulling the United States closer to open conflict with China and Russia. These subjects were of great interest in gatherings of both active duty officers and their retired colleagues.

Anderson attended one such gathering, the fiftieth reunion of the West Point Class of 1914. He received a kind note written on the back of a photo of the class taken at their twenty-fifth reunion in 1939. The note reads:

Oct 1, 1963

Dear Andy,

We were happy with each other on our 25th.

Let's warm the cockles of our hearts by being together again on our 50th

Please the many of us, who hold you in deep affection, by coming.

Charlie

Inscription on Invitation to West Point Class of 1914 50th Reunion, 1964

Dear Andy,

We were happy with each other on our 25th.
Let's warm the cockles of our hearts by being
together again on our 50th.
Please the many of us, who hold you in deep
affection, by coming.

Charlie , Charles M. Milliken,
his roommate from West Point.

This note is a sweet reminder of the feelings these old warriors
had for one another. Anderson made the effort to get to West Point
for his fiftieth reunion. Of the original 107 members of his class,
thirty-four attended the event.

There is no photo of this reunion in 1964; there is a roster with
Anderson's handwritten notes beside each member. Most classmates
were still alive, and all were retired from active duty. Some had died,
either in service to their country or by their own hand. The service
and fate of all the class members are noted in his handwriting and
likely were discussed and remembered that day.

Unlike many fiftieth college reunions where it is common to
fail to recognize the face and accomplishments of fellow classmates,
these men were intimately aware of each other's careers. Many had
served together, competed with one another, and fought alongside
one another. I believe all the members of Anderson's class would
have agreed with General Ernest Harmon's observations and hopes
for peace:

"As a professional soldier, I have always been one of
the true advocates of peace, because I realize perhaps
more than any other class of people the terrific waste,
misery and expenditure of war. I assure you, there
is nothing pretty about it, except the great spirit of
sacrifice and comradeship that is developed by the
men who have the dirty business to do."[87]

Of the class, twenty-seven of the cadets were promoted to general officer in their career (twenty-seven of 107 or 25 percent). Their ages ranged from sixty-eight to seventy-three years old. One member, Joseph Webster Allison, died during service after graduation on the Texas-Mexico border in the fight against Pancho Villa during the Mexican incursion. John Warren Weissheimer died in France during the First World War. Air accidents claimed the lives of John William Butts in 1919 in Americus, Georgia, and Sheldon Harley Wheeler in 1921 flying out of Luke Field in Hawaii. Wheeler Field at Pearl Harbor is named for Wheeler.[88]

General Vincente Lim, USMA 1914

A special note about Vincente P. Lim is appropriate. Although other foreign cadets had attended the Academy, Brigadier General Vincente Lim of the Philippines, nicknamed "Cannibal," was the first Filipino graduate of West Point, ranking seventy-seventh in the class of 107. He was an excellent shot, earning his Sharpshooter badge. He was not one to suffer insults lightly and was often punished for retaliating against slights and insults. Even during June Week, 1914, he was "walking the area" to work off demerits from a fight. In World War II, he led a guerilla force against the Japanese, was captured, and executed on December 31, 1944.

General Carl Spaatz, USMA 1914

There were two four-star generals in the class: Carl Andrew Spaatz of the Army Air Corps and Brehon Burke Somervell of the Army Corps of Engineers. Graduating ninety-seventh out of 107 in the class, General Spaatz's accomplishments included service with General John J. Pershing with the First Aero Squadron in 1915-1917 and the shooting down of three German planes in the last weeks of World War I. After a series of War Department assignments, he caught the eye of both Hap Arnold and George Marshall. As commander of Strategic Air Forces in Europe, he made bombing of German oil assets the number one priority of the Army Air Corps. He witnessed the

German surrender to the Americans at Reims, the German surrender to the Russians in Berlin, and the Japanese surrender to the Allies in Tokyo, the only man of general rank to witness in person all three surrender ceremonies.

General Brehon Somervell was the second four-star general in the Class of 1914. His engineering accomplishments were essential to the war effort. He was an Army Corps of Engineers officer and head of the Works Project Administration of New York City from 1936 to 1940. He headed up the construction of LaGuardia Airport. Because of his ability to deliver large engineering projects on time, he was given charge of the construction of the Pentagon, one of the most iconic and recognizable buildings in the world. He supervised 13,000 workers, who labored twenty-four hours a day, seven days a week, to complete the building in seven months. He was considered "a firecracker but ruthless" who "didn't care who he hit."[89]

In 1965, the nagging questions about the end of the war, of leaving Berlin to the Russians, and the relationships among top Allied commanders persisted. John Toland published his book *The Last 100 Days*.[90] The book rekindled many of the arguments from twenty years before. The controversy was the subject of a letter to the editor by General William H. Simpson published by the *New York Times* on June 12, 1966:

> *"I have read with considerable interest Brig. Gen. S.L.A. Marshall's[91] reviews of* The Last 100 Days *by John Toland and* The Last Battle *by Cornelius Ryan. I've always respected General Marshall's views and feel that throughout the years he has made a unique contribution to our military writing by his skillful recording of the actions of individuals and small units in combat, a field which had been neglected all too often in the past. Frankly, then, I was amazed to note in his interesting reviews of these two outstanding books several critical comments which, possibly through inadvertence or lack of factual knowledge, are misleading.*
>
> *"In his review of* The Last 100 Days, *he stated: 'Toland says quite flatly that the Americans would have captured Berlin had General Eisenhower not arbitrarily stopped his troops at the Elbe. To prove it, Toland quotes Gen. William*

H. Simpson, who commanded the US Ninth Army, which had one spearhead across the river at Barby, within less than 60 miles of Berlin, when the halt order came.'

"General Marshall then makes the following statement about me: 'Yet as one who was with that bridgehead force at the time, with the duty of determining the facts of the situation, I must reply that General Simpson's statement of how his troops stood when the halt was called is categorically wrong.' He then makes the following critical statement about the XIX Corps: 'The US XIX Corps, under Gen Raymond S. McLain, in the forefront of the Army, was spread out over 150 miles with its rear dangling in air and the Germans besetting it on front and both flanks.'

"In his review of The Last Battle,[92] *General Marshall makes the following critical statement: 'McLain's Corps was stretched out over 150 miles, beset on both flanks, with a real fire-fight going up front. Its logistical problems were heavy. Time was needed for collection and regrouping.'*

"I am unable to find in the two books any statement of mine as to how the Ninth Army troops stood when the halt was called. It does not follow, however, that I did not know. I think I knew as well as anyone else in the area at that time. As Commanding General of the US Ninth Army at the time, I must reply that I do not agree with either of General Marshall's statements quoted above. My answer to these statements is contained in the following statement of the general situation of the US Ninth Army on April 15, 1945.

"After crossing the Rhine River in March, 1945, the US Ninth Army, with its XIII and XIX Corps, advanced 226 miles in 19 days to reach the Elbe, some 50-60 miles from Berlin, on April 11, 1945. The only thing that moved faster than the Ninth Army in those days was a comparatively few fleeing remnants of the battered and broken German Army. I received the order to halt the US Ninth Army on the Elbe River on April 15, 1945. On that date, the Ninth Army consisted of three corps with three armored divisions, one airborne division (being used as an infantry division) and nine infantry divisions, a total of 13 divisions. The strength

of the Ninth Army during the advance from the Rhine to the Elbe averaged over 330,000 men daily. Morale and combat effectiveness were extremely high.

"In the XIX Corps zone, under General McLain, the 83d Infantry Division (less one regiment) had held a secure bridgehead since April 13 on the east side of the Elbe at Barby (about 15 miles south of Magdeburg). A combat command of the Second Armored Division was also in this bridgehead. A pontoon bridge which could carry all division loads was in operation. Preparations were being made to begin construction after nightfall on April 15 of a second bridge. On April 15 our troops holding the bridgehead attacked and expanded the bridgehead to an area of some 30 square miles. One infantry regimental combat team attached to the 83d Division began clearing, on April 15, the right flank of the corps between the Saale and Elbe Rivers. McLain also had the remainder of the Second Armored Division and a second infantry division on the Elbe River near Magdeburg.

"A third infantry division (less one regiment combat team) held the west bank of the Elbe from Tangermunde (about 30 miles north of Magdeburg) south to an area about 10 miles north of Magdeburg. A regiment of the 83d Division, which was mopping up in the Harz Mountains, and a combat command of the Eight Armored Division were protecting his right (south) flank. On April 15, no German forces west of the Elbe River were attacking or were capable of attacking either flank of the XIX Corps. With the exception of one infantry regiment in the Harz Mountains, the XIX Corps was closed up tight on the Elbe. The corps command post itself was at Wansleben, only about nine miles from the river. Very little, if any, time would have been needed for collection and regrouping. The corps was in excellent posture to continue on to Berlin.

"General Marshall probably was not in a position to know that the XIII Corps under Gen. Alvan C. Gillem Jr., had reached the Elbe at noon on April 12 at Tangermunde, just 53 miles from Berlin. On April 15 Gillem had one armored division and two infantry divisions on the west bank of the

Elbe north of Tangermunde. On April 15, his Fifth Armored Division was making plans for an assault over the river, execution of which could have been initiated that night. The XVI Corps, under Gen. John B. Anderson, with four divisions, had cleared the last resistance in the Ruhr Pocket on April 14. He had one additional division performing security missions. On April 15, the corps was regrouping and preparing for new duties including the release of forces for the Elbe River front. The Eighth Armored Division (less one combat command) was in the vicinity of Brunswick, in Army reserve.

"On April 15, the Ninth Army had two armored divisions and five infantry divisions, total seven division, on the Elbe River from the Barby area northwards with a secure bridgehead and a bridge at Barby. The entire Eighth Armored Division could have been assembled near Barby by daylight April 16 and thus raised the total number of divisions on the Elbe to eight on April 16.

"The initial operations east of the Elbe met with intense opposition. It is a matter of record that the three infantry battalions of the Second Armored Division in the northern bridgehead, which were unaccompanied by their tanks because of our inability to push over adequate bridging in that sector, were withdrawn on the 14th of April. Their losses were quite light, however. The units of the 83d Division in their bridgehead also met with considerable opposition initially. It is understandable that in the first few days of the fighting east of the Elbe some of the organization commanders may at times felt the situation to be extremely tenuous.

"The German units attacking the bridgehead were recently-formed divisions identified as Division Scharnhorst, Division Potsdam and Division Von Hutten. All were recently-formed scratch outfits at best. It was my estimate that the enemy resistance around the bridgehead was only a crust. In the advance to the Elbe quite a few pockets of enemy resistance were encountered, some of which put up a fairly stiff fight. The foremost divisions contained and by-passed these, knowing they would be taken care of by the units which followed. However, all of these defenses were comparatively

short-lived; the German forces had completely lost cohesion and the troops in the pockets had nowhere to go.

"The logistic support of the rapid movement eastward required careful initial planning and, at times, almost superhuman effort in execution. But the advance was never slowed down. The supply situation improved daily as rail lines were pushed forward east of the Rhine to take over some of the burden placed on the hundreds of trucks used to haul Army cargo. The Ninth Army logistic problems certainly were heavy, but they all were satisfactorily solved. During the period of operation to the Elbe, supplies were within reach of the using units at all times. At no time was the operation hampered by supply deficiencies. On April 15, the supply situation was good throughout the Army area. The US Ninth Army had ample supplies to drive and capture Berlin.

"By the 15th of April my estimate of the situation was that we could go on to Berlin if we were permitted to do so. This was based on the intelligence available to me at the time (which was subsequently confirmed), a careful review of the logistic situation and the considered opinions of my two corps commanders whose judgment I had never found to be wanting. There was no question in my mind but what we could do it, and do it economically with little loss.

"The Supreme Commander's decision to stop where we were was accepted by all in good grace, albeit with a certain amount of disappointment. How it all might have turned out had we gone on is, of course, a matter of conjecture. At the time, the feeling throughout the Ninth Army was that the Germans knew their collapse was imminent and that they would much prefer to surrender to us than to the Russians. I am convinced that the US Ninth Army could have captured Berlin well ahead of the Russians if it had not been stopped on the Elbe on 15 April, 1945."

This letter directly supports the argument that Berlin could have been captured by the Americans at the end of World War II. It does not address the human cost that effort would have been. It does state without question the conviction that the prize was within the grasp of the Western Allies. The geopolitical consequences of the capture and occupation of Berlin and the territories west of the city have been the subject of considerable speculation and conjecture. What is likely true is that the 1949 Berlin Airlift and the 1961 Berlin Wall would not have occurred. The lives of Allied aviators in the Berlin Airlift would not have been lost, the people of Berlin would have been spared months of uncertainty and deprivation, and the tyranny of the wall to hold the East Berliners captive would have been avoided.

General Anderson in Retirement on Albemarle Street, Washington DC, Christmas 1963

For General Anderson, the years continued to roll away. The XVI Corps' annual reunion had devolved into a small dinner at the Army-Navy Club in Washington, DC. At the gathering in March 1966, Anderson was presented a sterling service tray. The tray was engraved with the XVI Corps emblem "front and center." The occasion was especially notable—it was Anderson's seventy-fifth birthday. For the remainder of his life, the tray resided on a table in the front hall of his home, for calling cards and such.

In the spring of 1968, his health took a turn for the worse. For years he had listened patiently to the doctors' admonitions to moderate his alcohol intake and nicotine use. Then the roof caved in. In early June 1968, he suffered a stroke that left him unable to speak clearly nor use his right arm and leg. In those days, there was no rushing off to the hospital, no antiplatelet therapy, no thrombolytic therapy, or CAT scans. It was early summer, hot and sticky in Washington. He was bedridden, in the "Palmer" bed, a four-poster bed of enormous size that filled the upstairs bedroom and required a four-step stepstool to get high enough to climb under the sheets.

Not three months before, he had sat with his grandsons, Scott, John, and Michael, making a tape about his early career. The boys had "planned," as adolescent boys do, to resume the recording session later. Like most adolescent boys, they thought that there would be time.

In the summer of 1972, Mrs. Anderson broke her hip. She was hospitalized at Sibley Memorial Hospital off of Reservoir Road in northwest Washington. It was a big blow to her entire family. Whereas General Anderson had recovered enough to go out to dinner, Mrs. Anderson was disabled terribly by the two operations she needed that year. With her disability, General Anderson became increasingly reclusive.

The remainder of his life was a downward spiral, the so-called "Arlington Curve," a term used by resident physicians at the military hospitals in the Washington area to describe the downward trajectory of old soldiers and sailors under their care. The "curve" is the DC beltway, the road around the District of Columbia that leads from Walter Reed and Bethesda Naval Hospital to Arlington National Cemetery.

Chapter 15

SOLDIER OF THE GREAT WAR

Major General John Benjamin Anderson died September 1, 1976, and was buried at Arlington National Cemetery with full military honors. Mrs. Anderson, her daughter, son-in-law Smilin' Jack Van Ness, and the author drove silently together in the car to Arlington. It was a typical muggy Washington summer day, the hot air still and heavy with humidity, even in the late morning. Just exiting the car in that heat started a sweat under the collar. As Mrs. Anderson shuffled and stumbled from the car to the gravesite, Michael helped her along. Sweat rolled down between his shoulder blades, contributing to his anxiety and sadness.

As a major general, Anderson rated a funeral service at the Old Post Chapel at Fort Myer, but none was performed. Instead, the family met the casket at the gravesite. The horse-drawn caisson with the riderless horse stood on the road off in the distance. Pershing's Own remained at "parade rest." No procession nor muffled drums. No ceremony beyond the bare minimum. No time for reflection nor time to honor General Anderson's thirty-six years of service. Mrs. Anderson and Tudy were in such a state of anxiety and grief that they could only think to do their duty and get the funeral behind them as quickly as possible.

The preparations were perfunctory and rushed. The other grandsons were absent. Scott was on active duty with the US Army in Germany; at the time of his grandfather's death, he was on leave, but the address he had given lacked sufficient detail to contact him to return. John was in college in Florida and could not return. Other family members, XVI Corps veterans and friends, and West Point classmates and spouses were likewise absent.

A sparse crowd of official mourners, "Arlington ladies," and Army staffers were the only other attendees. No veterans of the 102nd, no comrades from West Point's Class of 1914 or the West Point Club of Washington. General and Mrs. Anderson had become recluses; they were no longer in contact with their circle of friends from the Army days.

The ceremony commenced without fanfare and proceeded perfunctorily. The duty chaplain spoke of my grandfather's service in the most general, banal terms. He knew nothing of his Iowa origin, his Mexico service, nor his time in the Philippines. He mentioned his World War II service but was confused about the details. It was a "canned" eulogy—uninspiring.

Then came the playing of taps. The notes stirred powerful feelings; the forty-three-note melody meant that General Anderson was dead—like so many soldiers before him laid to rest after taps. The three rapid, sharp cracks of rifle volleys snapped the family out of their musings and introspection. Then came the thirteen-gun salute, the United States' final salute to a major general.

Arrayed on the road adjacent to Section 10 of Arlington National Cemetery, the guns banged away and the smoke hung in the thick air. It clung to us at the gravesite and obscured our view of Washington, the Pentagon, and the other graves. The gunpowder smoke smelled of fireworks on the Fourth of July, the rifle range at camp, and childhood fun—just a hint of danger, an unexpected shell burst, the rattle of rifle fire, or the "whiff of the grape." For the small crowd, it gave a hint of the romance and traditions of military life. The breeze picked up, and the smoke swirled away from us.

The smoke drifted across the hills of Arlington, carried away to the graves of my grandfather's classmates and comrades-in-arms. To General John J. Pershing, his first commanding officer on the Texas-Mexico border. To General Joe Swing, his motorcycle companion racing around the villages of France in World War I. To General

Alvan Gillem, XIII Corps commander, the gracious and affable host of many luncheons and conferences of comrades prior to the Rhine River crossing. And finally down the hill to the final resting place of his great friend and mentor, General William H. Simpson, commanding general, US Ninth Army, with whom he crossed the Rhine with Winston Churchill.

All of them were in their final resting place together. They had served in faraway lands and at home in the service of their country; they had borne together the responsibilities of war and peace; they had made decisions together that affected the lives of their men; they had faced together enemies intent on doing harm to themselves and the country; and they had fought together and against one another for command and for recognition. How fitting that they now were buried together.

Twenty years later, General Anderson's son-in-law, Smilin' Jack, wrote a letter to his sons outlining his requests for his own Arlington funeral. Smilin' Jack Van Ness wanted full military honors, a chapel service, and the long march with the horse-drawn caisson accompanied by Pershing's Own. He wanted his Arlington funeral to be a time of remembrance, joy, and celebration. He did not want the occasion to be one of sadness or regret. He wanted the family to have time to reflect, to consider his service and sacrifice and, by extension, honor the service of all his family. He wanted his own celebrant, his second cousin, the Reverend Katherine Megee Lehman, the granddaughter of his mother's brother. Reverend Lehman knew Smilin' Jack as "Harper"; the family came to know her as "Kitty."

Smilin' Jack died in the spring of 2007. The family honored his request to be buried at Arlington with full military honors. Even though the waiting list was three months' long, arrangements were made to have a simple Episcopalian service at the Old Post Chapel at Fort Myer, Virginia. A program incorporating the embossed "Wings of Gold" of a Naval Aviator was produced.

In the Old Post Chapel outside Arlington National Cemetery, the Reverend Lehman, in her black robe and stiff clerical collar and hair pulled back into a ponytail without a strand out of place, stood high up in the pulpit and looked down on the gathering seated in the hard, wooden pews. Family, friends, wives, children, classmates, and shipmates were gathered there. My father's flag-draped casket was carried in by six muscular and immaculately dressed "squared away" sailors. The casket rested on a simple bier in the center aisle at the front of the chapel.

"Kitty" Lehman looked down on our upturned faces and gently met our eyes. She smiled graciously. Her calmness was reassuring. It would be OK. Praising God, "Alleluia," she turned from the simple wooden altar with its gold cross and began her eulogy:

> *"We cannot adequately attend to our response to this place and to this occasion without asking its larger meaning. We are here to remember and to pray, amidst the fallen. What can be the meaning of so many lives lost in this war-torn world, in this endless struggle between love and fear? Have we come far enough yet, in our restless pursuit of justice and peace, to confirm their sacrifice? I find it most genuinely helpful to admit that we don't know. Still, the clearest triumph is that we hold life most precious.*
>
> *"Some years ago, I picked up a book by Mark Helprin. Actually, I got it for my husband, himself a naval aviator during the Vietnam War. The novel was about the Alpini during World War I, or at least I thought it was. As sometimes happens, I ended up reading it before my husband got around to it. The title is* A Soldier of the Great War.[93] *Like all fine literature, it turned out to be about life. World War I was simply the backdrop and the metaphor. The Great War turned out to be life itself. Harper was a sailor and an aviator of the greatest war of all, the battle for life's ultimate meaning. And so are we all soldiers of that great war.*
>
> *"It is in places like this and at times like this that we pause to consider in awe and reverence all that is of greatest value to us in this life. We recommit our own lives to serve those goods above all else. We express our intuition that such great goods are enduring in a more transcendent sense than we can even imagine. And in so doing, we define ourselves, and we shape the world for future generations.*
>
> *"For Harper, the overriding goods were family, friends, and community, lived out in service to country, to the wonders of science and technology, and to the ultimate mystery we*

term God, the benevolence that we hope and trust comprises the very core and extent of all things, of inner and outer space. That was the sermon Harper preached with his life. It remains for each of us to preach our own. May we do as well. AMEN."

Reverend Lehman's eulogy for Harper "Smilin' Jack" were the words my family needed at my Father's funeral, and wish we had at my Grandfather's service. The message of hope, devotion, and duty comforted and inspired us. The words reminded us that the mysteries of life are often beyond ready understanding. While my grandfather's life played out at the highest level of responsibility and power, it had meaning and purpose beyond his military service. The love of his wife as revealed in his wartime letters, his devotion to West Point classmates and friends as revealed in photos and keepsakes, and his commitment to quiet tasks as revealed in his smile, the twinkle in his eye, and the warmth of his words are his enduring legacy. No uniform, medal, or official recognition is more important than the quiet grace and humility General John B. Anderson displayed in his declining years.

EPILOGUE

Recently, the author had occasion to be reminded of the depth of feeling and the appreciation, not just of the citizens of Roermond, but of the Dutch people in general, for the events of 1945. Some seventy-five years after the fact, while traveling in Botswana, a Dutch couple joined a group around a campfire in the Kalahari Desert. As happens on safari, stories were exchanged and family histories recounted. Some of General Anderson's history was shared, but it was just one story among many shared that evening under the canopy of stars of the southern hemisphere, miles removed from the battlefields of Europe of 1945.

The next day, as the Dutchman prepared to depart, he pulled me away from the group for a private word. Gripping my hand firmly, first with one and then with both hands, firmly, and with a penetrating look in his eyes, the Dutchman thanked me for my grandfather's efforts on behalf of his countrymen, in a time long ago, in a place far away.

For more information on the life of Major General John B. Anderson, especially our request to the Army Board of Corrections for posthumous promotion of Major General Anderson to the rank of Lieutenant General, go to the author's website, www. drmichaelvanness.com.

ENDNOTES

CHAPTER 1

[1]   His mother Louise (Kirstine Frederikke Lovise Simonsen) was born April 24, 1844, in Sejlstrup, Denmark. Her parents were Hans Simonsen and Anthonette Dichmann. She was the sixth oldest of thirteen children and grew up on a farm in northern Denmark. She died June 22, 1913, and is buried in Oak Hill Cemetery in Parkersburg, Iowa. Louise Simonsen's first marriage was to Thomas Jensen in the early 1860s. They had one son, Frederik Andreas Jensen, born in 1865. Thomas Jensen died sometime between 1865 and 1869. Louise Simonsen remarried to Carl Christian Anderson (Kristian Karl Andersen) on October 29, 1869, and immigrated to Iowa about 1882. Frederik Jensen immigrated to Iowa with his mother and stepfather and lived in rural Franklin County, Iowa, just west of the city of Hampton, then settled in Parkersburg, Iowa. Carl Anderson is listed in census records as a "laborer." Carl and Louise Anderson had six children—four daughters and two sons. Carl Anderson died January 18, 1917, and is buried in Oak Hill Cemetery in Parkersburg.

[2]   Hanna Anderson (Johanna Antoinette Andersen) was the eldest daughter of Carl and Louise Anderson. She was born in Sejlstrup, Denmark. She immigrated with her parents to Iowa in 1882. Later in life she lived in Chicago.

Symona Marie Anderson (Marie Simone Andersen) was the second daughter of Carl and Louise Anderson. She was born in Sejlstrup, Denmark, and immigrated to Iowa in 1882. She married Edward Charles Allen on March 22, 1892, in Ackley, Iowa. They had five children: William, Harry, Allene, Arthur, and Ruth. As a consequence of Edward's alcoholism, Symona and Edward Allen divorced in 1910 and neither ever remarried. Nels D. Anderson (Niels

D. Andersen) was the eldest son of Carl and Louise Anderson. He was born May 24, 1876, in Borglum, Denmark. He immigrated with his parents to the United States in 1882. He lived in Franklin County, Iowa, and Parkersburg, Iowa, in the late 1800s and early 1900s. He joined the US Army and married Jennie Freund in the early 1910s. He lived in California (San Francisco and Sacramento) from the early 1900s until his death on May 16, 1942. Nels and Jennie Anderson had one son, Carl, born 1913.

Amelia Elizabeth Anderson (Emilie Elisabeth Andersen) was the third daughter of Carl and Louise Anderson. She was named after her aunt Amelia Simonsen, who immigrated to the United States in 1883 and lived in Parkersburg, Iowa, until her death in the 1920s. Amelia Anderson married John S. Richardson Jr. on June 4, 1902. They produced two children, John Gerald Richardson (1903-1991) and Katherine Louise Richardson (1907-1993). Amelia and John S. Richardson are buried in Oak Hill Cemetery, Parkersburg, Iowa, in a grave adjacent to Carl and Louise Anderson.

Margaret Anderson was born in rural Franklin County, Iowa, on August 17, 1882. The family moved to Parkersburg, Iowa, shortly after she was born. She married Henry Janssen Johnson Jr. in the early 1900s. Henry and Margaret had one son, Robert Johnson, born 1911. It was to her that Captain John B. Anderson wished his personal effects sent in the event of his death in the trenches of France in World War I. She died in 1971 and is buried next to her husband in Oak Hill Cemetery, Parkersburg, Iowa.

CHAPTER 2

[3]   Charlie the Barber was popular among the cadets and a rabid fan of the Eastern Division New York Giants.

CHAPTER 4

[4]   The *U.S.S. Henry R. Mallory* was eventually sunk by a German U-boat off the coast of Iceland in 1943.

[5]   Captain Ralph Heard, ed., *Sixth Regiment Field Artillery* (Germany: Coblenz, 1919).

[6]   Four divisions of the Canadian Corps relieved II Anzac Corps in October 1917 in the same area occupied by the First Canadian Division in April 1915.

[7]   Lieutenant General Godley was a controversial figure in the history of the British Army. He served often with New Zealand and Australian troops. He was at Gallipoli and was felt to be cavalier with the lives of colonial troops. Despite these criticisms, he remained in command of British and colonial troops on the Western Front. In retirement, he remained active and was even called back in 1939 at the age of seventy-two to command Home Guard troops in London. He was the epitome of an austere and resolute Englishman.

[8]   Captain Ralph T. Heard, ed., *Sixth Regiment Field Artillery* (Germany: Coblenz, 1919).

CHAPTER 5

[9]   Lucius Henry Chappell, president of the Columbus Historical Society, 1916-1918.

[10]   *USAT Thomas* was a US Army transport ship named for General George Henry Thomas, hero of the Civil War battle of Chickamauga. Mainly used on the Manila run, *USAT Thomas* made her last run in March 1928.

[11]   Isabel and Duff were Sue Anderson's sister-in-law and brother, respectively. Their two boys were George and Martin.

[12]   The San Francisco earthquake was a 7.9 magnitude event that struck at five a.m. on April 18. Within three days, more than thirty fires from ruptured gas mains consumed 80 percent of the city, causing 3,000 deaths. More than 75 percent of the 400,000 inhabitants were left homeless.

[13]   Carl Anderson was Nels' Anderson's only son, born 1913.

[14]   This initial step taken by Adolf Hitler to restore Germany's "rightful" place in the nations of Europe included cessation of payment of reparations for WWI, the occupation of the Rhineland, and the resumption of pilot flight training. When the Western Powers failed to respond to these actions, Hitler began to take increasingly aggressive steps.

CHAPTER 6

[15] Aide-de-Camp Guy R. McFall of Pickens, South Carolina.

[16] Wife of General Anderson's Chief of Staff George Keyser.

[17] Mr. Fleming was a partner of the firm Folger, Nolan, Fleming, and Douglas, an established investment banking house of Washington, DC.

[18] The Senator Elmer Thomas referred to in the letter was the senior Oklahoma senator at the time having been elected in 1926. He was interested in international affairs and supported the League of Nations, the Kellogg-Briand Peace Pact, and the World Court. He voted for neutrality in 1935 and 1937, saying the United States was unprepared for war. After becoming chair of the Sub-Committee on Military Appropriations in 1938, he toured the country and stated that our country's defenses were "in critical condition."

[19] Wife of Division Artillery Commander, Brigadier General Charles M. Busbee.

[20] Lieutenant Colonel Callie H. Palmer, Camp Maxey camp commander, played an important role in the development of the new 102nd Infantry Division. He would soon present the regimental unit commanders with their regimental colors and the commanding officer the division standards for the new 102nd Infantry Division.

[21] Courtney Hodges was a "mustang" officer rising through the ranks from private to four-star general, commanding general of the US First Army.

[22] Brigadier General Alonzo "Pat" Fox served as the 102nd Division assistant commander with General Anderson. He was a graduate of St. Louis University.

[23] Bradford G. Chynoweth, *Bellamy Park* (Hicksville, New York: Exposition Press, 1975), 120.

CHAPTER 7

[24] Robert Berlin, "Corps in Combat," *The Journal of Military History*, no. 53 (1989): 147.

[25]   Matthew B. Ridgway, *Soldier: The Memoirs of Matthew B. Ridgway* (New York: Harper, 1956), 18.

[26]   Charles H. Corlett, *Cowboy Pete: An Autobiography of Major General Charles H. Corlett* (Santa Fe, New Mexico: Sleeping Fox Publishers, 1974), 25.

[27]   United States Military Academy, *The Howitzer* (1915): 55.

[28]   United States Military Academy, *The Howitzer* (1917): 50.

[29]   Edward Brooks was a combat leader who led the Second Armored Division in Normandy and the VI Corps in France and Germany. He retired as a lieutenant general.

[30]   General Gillem was the commanding general of the II Armored Corps at Fort Knox and later the US XIII Corps of the US Ninth Army.

[31]   Colonel George R. Barker was born in Atlanta, Georgia, on February 16, 1894. He attended Marist Military College and the Georgia School of Technology. Upon graduation, he was commissioned as a second lieutenant of Cavalry on March 22, 1917, and served in Panama from 1920 to 1923. During the interwar years he attended the Advanced Course at Fort Benning and the Command and General Staff School at Fort Leavenworth, Kansas. Prior to assignment to the XVI Corps, he served as chief of staff of the VIII Corps and assisted in the organization of the XVI Corps.

[32]   Lieutenant Colonel Harold A. Furlong was a Medal of Honor recipient for actions in combat in the First World War. During the Battle of Meuse-Argonne, he crossed open ground under fire, took a position behind a line of German machine gun nests, killed several German gunners, and captured an additional twenty German soldiers. He was presented the Congressional Medal of Honor by General John J. Pershing. He was one of only 121 Medal of Honor recipients in World War I.

[33]   This camp was established in 1941 by the commander of the Army Ground Forces, Lieutenant General Lesley McNair. The first division to undergo winter maneuvers at Watersmeet on the Michigan Upper Peninsula was the Second Infantry Division in 1942.

[34]   "Necessary Risk: Churchill at the Front. Brendan Bracken's Defense." Winston Churchill Project at Hillsdale College, December 11, 2017. This

article was published by Hillsdale College as part of its teaching mission to understand statesmanship and leadership.

[35]   Stephen R. Taafe, *Marshall and His Generals: U.S. Army Commanders in World War II* (Lawrence, Kansas: University Press of Kansas, 2011), 246.

[36]   Dwight D. Eisenhower, *Crusade in Europe* (Garden City, New York: Doubleday, 1948), 376.

[37]   John A. English, *Patton's Peers: The Forgotten Allied Field Army Commanders of the Western Front, 1944-45* (Mechanicsburg, Pennsylvania: Stackpole Press, 2009), 141.

[38]   Russell F. Weigley, *Eisenhower's Lieutenants: The Campaigns of France and Germany, 1944-1945* (Bloomington, Indiana: University Press, 1981), 431.

[39]   John A. English, *Patton's Peers: The Forgotten Allied Field Army Commanders of the Western Front, 1944-45* (Mechanicsburg, Pennsylvania, Stackpole Press, 2009), 141.

[40]   Alvan C. Gillem Jr., "William H. Simpson," *Leadership at Higher Levels of Command as Viewed by Senior and Experienced Combat Commanders* (Monterey: USALRU, 1961): 26. This article was cited by Jerry D. Morelock, *Generals of the Bulge* (Mechanicsburg, Pennsylvania: Stackpole Books, 2015), 140.

[41]   Red Ball Express was an emergency measure taken by the Twelfth Army Group. Drivers were primarily African American. The program stripped two-and-a-half ton trucks from field artillery, tank destroyer, and anti-aircraft units to form truck companies that operated day and night on highways restricted to their use to deliver vital supplies.

[42]   "Doc" Cook was one of the US Army corps commanders who was relieved from duty. In his case, the pain of peripheral vascular disease, likely a consequence of chronic tobacco use, disabled him from further service in the field.

[43]   Major General Cook's XII Corps was given to Major General Manton Eddy, a cautious infantryman who came to appreciate General Patton's aggressive cavalry-like advances into German lines. Under Major General

Eddy, the armor-heavy XII Corps with the Fourth and Sixth Armored divisions came to be known as the "Spearhead of Patton's Third Army."

CHAPTER 8

[44]   Carlo D'Este, *Eisenhower: A Soldier's Life* (New York: Henry Holt and Company, 2002), 638.

[45]   Margaret was one of General Anderson's older sisters.

[46]   Colonel George Barker was chief of staff of the XVI Corps.

[47]   It is family lore that during the First World War, General Anderson received the proverbial "Dear John" letter while serving near Ypres attached to the British Expeditionary Force. If so, one can understand his apparent interest in continued receipt of letters from home.

[48]   General Terry de la Mesa Allen's career, with its many ups and downs, demonstrates the difficulty the Army Chief of Staff George Marshall and other senior commanders had in balancing the need for general officers capable of fighting aggressively and the requirements of Army discipline. General Allen was born in Utah and attended West Point but was dismissed. After obtaining his bachelor's degree from Catholic University in 1912, he rejoined the Army, served in World War I, attended both the US Army Cavalry School at Fort Riley and the US Army Infantry School at Fort Benning, and took the US Army Command and General Staff course at Fort Leavenworth. Given command of the First Infantry Division in 1942, he led the unit through North Africa. The First Infantry Division took part in Operation Torch, the invasion of North Africa in November 1942. Parts of the division were involved in the major actions across northern Africa, including the defeat at the Battle of Kasserine Pass. Gathering their legs underneath them, the First Infantry Division under General Allen led the Allied assault and victory in El Guettar, Geja, and Mateur. After almost six months of continual combat, the First Infantry Division led the capture of nearly 250,000 Axis combatants. After the fighting of the previous six months, they had only a short respite. The talents of both General Allen and his assistant division commander Theodore Roosevelt Jr. as combat leaders were widely recognized. They had won the fight. Their officers and soldiers adored them.

Unfortunately, First Division soldiers ran amok in the wake of their victory in Tunisia. Drunken brawls, ransacked bars and cafes, and disorderly conduct among the enlisted ranks and young officers was witnessed by many and was not discouraged by their superiors. They had won a fight against the Italians and their German allies, a fight that had started out badly and which many thought the US Army was not capable of winning. Their conduct after the victory in Tunisia was felt "unbecoming" of soldiers of the United States Army.

Omar Bradley blamed Generals Allen and Roosevelt. He felt that they did not possess the instincts of good disciplinarians and had let them loose on unsuspecting civilians. The behavior of the soldiers under their command was considered an embarrassment. Thus, upon learning of the drunken behavior of the First Division soldiers, Omar Bradley recommended Allen's relief as commanding general of the First Division. Major General Clarence R. Huebner assumed command.

Although relieved of command of the First Infantry Division, General Allen's reputation for being a fighter lived on. He was given command of a new division, a new outfit—the 104th Infantry Division, the "Timberwolves." Starting from scratch and likely applying the lessons learned in combat in North Africa, he created fighters in his new division, which soon was ranked with the best. Omar Bradley, who had relieved Allen two years before for the drunken behavior and undisciplined actions of his men, complimented Major General Allen, saying "these young Timberwolves of yours already rank along with the First and Ninth infantry divisions as the finest assault divisions in the ETO (European theater of operations)."

[49]   Malin Craig Jr. letter, 1969, reads in part, "On December 12th, 1944, the new 106th Division took over the area from the 2nd Division, which was ordered to the Hurtgen Forrest, 50 to 75 kilometers to the north. The Commanding General of the 106th Division was ordered to occupy the lines of the 2nd Division 'man for man and gun for gun,' meaning that no intelligent rearrangement of forces or positions was to be permitted. General Alan W. Jones, commanding the 106th Division, protested vigorously. The lines of the Siegfried bulged far to the east at this point, adding very materially to the long front of the Division. About seven or eight kilometers to the west lies a stronger defensive position, with no dangerous road net behind it—altogether an incomparably superior position for units temporarily on the defense.

"General Jones' recommendations were disregarded, and the orders were repeated: 'relieve the 2nd Division man for man and gun for gun', with only a lame explanation that the 2nd Division was much more experienced.

"On 16 December, the Germans attacked at 5:00 in the morning. Within 48 hours the two northern combat teams had been surrounded, badly cut up, and forced to surrender or starve. A few daring groups succeeded in finding their ways through the thick woods and strong forces of Germans, but about 9200 of the 13,000 members of the Division were killed or captured before the Division had been in the lines a week.

"I met General Robertson in Hawaii in 1948, and tactfully asked him as to the disposition of the 2nd Division when the 106th took over the lines. He informed me as follows.

"Shortly after the advance came to a halt, in the summer or early fall of 1944, General Eisenhower visited the 2nd Division sector. General Robertson informed him that he intended to rearrange his lines for defense (a precaution that has been standard operating procedure among military men through all history). General Eisenhower instructed him to remain as he was, that he was not to withdraw from the Siegfried Line, which would be poor newspaper publicity. General Robertson was still very bitter about it when I discussed it with him, three or four years later."

[50]   In December 1943, General Anderson was still the commanding officer of the 102nd Infantry Division, which participated along with the Eighty-fourth, Ninety-ninth, and 103rd infantry divisions in recently completed maneuvers conducted by and "won" by General Krueger's Third Army.

[51]   General Anderson was unable to relate the events of the previous nine days in this letter. With the beginning of what became known as the Battle of the Bulge, as alluded to above, all US forces improvised and reacted to the ever-changing conditions of the battle. For example, the plan for the XVI Corps to relieve the British XII Corps on the line on December 16 in a sector adjacent to the US Ninth Army area was scrapped and the planning group was recalled; the XVI Corps Artillery Fire Direction Center was made operational at Elmendorf, Germany, and was put under the control of the XIII Corps Artillery commander. Major General Anderson would be ordered to Headquarters, XVIII Airborne Corps in the Ardennes as deputy

corps commander on December 26, 1944. These actions cannibalized the XVI Corps headquarters unit and delayed the formal activation of the XVI Corps headquarters as an independent, functional entity. Although General Anderson returned to his command on December 29, 1944, headquarters personnel from the G-2, G-3, Signal, and Artillery sections remained with the XVIII Airborne Corps until January 9, 1945.

[52]   Major General William Kean, chief of staff for Courtney Hodges' First Army, was a USMA '18 graduate.

[53]   Both Generals Stanford and Prickett were relieved of command by General Hodges on January 23, 1945 as the Seventy-fifth Division was not performing up to General Hodges' expectations.

[54]   Katherine Cornell was an American stage actress, born in Berlin, Germany, and raised in Buffalo, New York. She was regarded as one of the great actresses of the day. Her most famous role was the one she performed in Europe for the troops, the role of the English poet Elizabeth Barrett Browning. A stage actress regarded mainly as a tragedienne, she appeared in only one film, *Stage Door Canteen*, a World War II morale booster in which she played herself. She was considered a refined, romantic actress, subtle in her theatrical skills and romanticism. I can understand General Anderson's excitement and enjoyment of her company, an interlude from the difficulties of war. I can also understand his efforts to include his wife and daughter in the pleasure of the dinner event.

[55]   General Paschal was relieved from command of the Seventy-fifth Infantry Division by General Matthew Ridgway. The loss of command was the sad end to an extraordinary Army career. As a first lieutenant in World War I, Brigadier General Paul Paschal, USMA '14, was awarded the Distinguished Service Cross for extraordinary heroism in action in the Bois d'Aigremont, France, July 15, 1918.

CHAPTER 9

[56]   The "Marlene" referred to in the letter is Marlene Dietrich, the German-born actress of stage and film fame. During the 1930s she made several films like *The Blue Angel, Morocco, Shanghai Express,* and *Desire* that brought her

international fame and recognition. She was glamorous and exotic in her looks and demeanor. Throughout World War II, she worked diligently to improve the morale of Allied soldiers and the living conditions of refugees from both France and Germany. She visited the front line so many times that the director Billy Wilder commented, "She was at the front lines more than Eisenhower." She recorded songs as part of the Musak project, an Office of Strategic Services program to demoralize German soldiers. Her most memorable song was "Lili Marlene"—a favorite of both the Germans and Americans.

[57]   Kaldenkirchen, Germany, is located in the North Rhine-Westphalia area of Germany, close to the border at Venlo. After crossing the Roer River, troops of the XVI Corps renamed the main street in honor of their commander. Sometime after the war, the sign honoring General Anderson was removed and lost. The street has been renamed.

CHAPTER 10

[58]   Charles B. McDonald, *United States Army in World War II: The European Theater of Operations—The Last Offensive* (Atlanta, Georgia: Whitman Publishing, 2012), 304.

[59]   Arthur Bryant, *Triumph in the West: Completing the War Diaries of Field Marshall Viscount Alanbrooke* (London: Collins, 1959), 436.

[60]   Henry G. Wales was a war correspondent during the First and Second World Wars. He was well known for his detailed and complete recitation of the facts of momentous events. He was present at the execution of the spy for the Axis, Mata Hari, on October 18, 1917, at Vincennes Barracks in France. By the time he witnessed the Rhine River crossing, he was experienced and senior to most of his reporter colleagues. Examples of his work are included in the book *Dispatches from the Front: A History of the American War Correspondent* by Nathaniel Lande.

[61]   David Irving, *The War Between the Generals* (New York: Houghton Mifflin, 1981), 398. Kay Summersby departed by car the next morning. The relationship between Dwight Eisenhower and its effect on his decision making has been the subject of much speculation. At a time of increasing

command responsibility and fatigue, Eisenhower had his hands full.

[62]   Robert C. Stern, *US Navy and the War in Europe* (S. Yorkshire, Great Britain: Seaforth Publishing, 2012), 218.

[63]   Arthur Bryant, *Triumph in the West: Completing the War Diaries of Field Marshall Viscount Alanbrooke* (London: Collins, 1959).

[64]   D-Day is a military term used to denote any "Decision Day" like the Normandy landings on June 6, 1944, or the Rhine River crossing.

[65]   Johnny Chickering, a native of Washington DC, was a handsome and athletic gymnast at West Point who graduated in the Class of '45. He served as a fighter pilot in Korea before working at NASA headquarters in the 1960s.

[66]   Tommy Donaldson was Thomas Quinton Donaldson, USMA, in Johnnie Devine's Eighth Armored Division, under General Anderson's XVI Corps command.

CHAPTER 11

[67]   Omar N. Bradley, *A Soldier's Story* (New York: Henry Holt and Company, 1951).

[68]   James Lester was a classmate at West Point, Class of 1914, and commanded the Ninety-sixth Infantry Division during the invasion of Okinawa. The Ninety-sixth received the Presidential Unit Citation for its extraordinary heroism during the battle and is one of only four entire Army divisions in WWII to receive this distinction. Lewis Pick was a 1914 graduate of the Virginia Polytechnic Institute and received a Regular Army commission in 1917. He crossed paths with General Anderson in the Philippines in the 1920s. During the Second World War, he was assigned to the China Burma India Theater and oversaw construction of the vital Ledo Road, nicknamed "Pick's Pike," General Joseph Stilwell's highway from India through North Burma to China.

[69]   Franz von Papen was a German nobleman, German staff officer, politician, and ambassador. At the beginning of World War I, he was the military attaché in Washington. Suspected of espionage and acts of sabotage, he was sent

back to Germany in 1915. In the 1920s, as an ultra-right-wing member of the monarchist Catholic Center Party, he served as deputy of the Prussian Landtag. In the early 1930s, he played a significant role in dissolving the Weimar Republic. In 1932, he was elevated to the chancellorship of Germany by President Paul von Hindenburg. After a political coup by elements of the government opposed to his authoritarian methods, he resigned and threw his support behind Adolf Hitler for chancellor of Germany. As vice chancellor, he naively believed he had the support of enough non-Nazi political leaders to restrain Hitler. He was appointed ambassador to Austria before its annexation into the Third Reich.

70   Brigadier General Ralph McTyeire Pennell, USMA '14, was serving as the commanding general of the Field Artillery School at Fort Sill, Oklahoma, at the time of this visit and would have likely been aware of the discussions of Pacific commanders.

71   Omar N. Bradley, *A Soldier's Story* (New York: Henry Holt and Company, 1951), 535.

72   Undersecretary of War Robert P. Patterson was an active supporter of the Army and worked tirelessly to prepare and support the men in the field. He was a veteran of World War I. He reached the rank of major and received both the Distinguished Service Cross and Silver Star for heroism for actions with the Seventy-seventh Infantry Division. A respected jurist, appointed to the United States Court of Appeals for the Second Circuit by President Roosevelt, he left the bench to join the War Department.

73   Ham Wade Hampton Haislip, USMA '12, was born in Woodstock, Virginia, in July 1889, and named for Confederate General Wade Hampton of the Army of Northern Virginia. General Haislip served as commanding general of the Eighty-fifth Infantry Division, the XV Corps, and the Seventh Army. He was vice chief of staff of the United States Army from 1949-1951. He was the recipient of four Distinguished Service Medals. While stationed at Fort Sam Houston, he introduced Mamie Doud to her future husband, Dwight Eisenhower. He served as a pall bearer at Eisenhower's funeral.

CHAPTER 12

[75]   In a US Army hospital in Italy in 1943, a violinist dressed in military fatigues entered to play for wounded soldiers. As he entered, one man who had lost his right arm tried to applaud. With his left hand in the air, he smiled and clapped as best he could. The violinist was temporarily shocked. Although he had played in many military hospitals, nothing had prepared him for that moment. He was accompanied that day by his pianist, Milton Kaye. More than fifty years later, Kaye recalls Heifetz' words: "You see, this is why we play."

Jascha Heifetz was in Beckum, Germany, on May 8, 1945, the day the war ended. Born in Russian Lithuania in 1901, Heifetz had come to the United States at age sixteen and became a citizen in 1925. He was considered by many the greatest violinist of the twentieth century. He gave a VE-Day concert in Beckum. One week later, he was asked by Omar Bradley to perform at a banquet honoring the Russian general Marshal Ivan K, commander of the First Ukrainian Army Group. The actor Mickey Rooney and the Glenn Miller Orchestra joined him in the German spa town of Bad Wildungen. They played five selections, starting with Heifetz's arrangement of the spiritual "Deep River" and ending with Prokofiev's "March from the Love of Three Oranges." He was mobbed by GIs who asked for his autograph on captured German marks. His accompanist that day was seventeen-year-old Seymour Lipkin, who had trained at the Curtis Institute of Music in Philadelphia.

[76]   The emergency of the Battle of the Bulge disrupted the command arrangements planned before the German attack. The Seventh-fifth, Seventy-eighth, and 106th infantry divisions were assigned to the First Army in an effort to stem the German advance. Since the XVI Corps was part of the US Ninth Army, with the assignment of these three divisions to the First Army, the XVI Corps was "without a job."

[77]   Major General Leroy "Wap" H. Watson, USMA '15, was a classmate of Dwight Eisenhower at West Point and a year junior to General Anderson. Major General Watson had commanded the Third Armored Division in Normandy in June 1944. However, as a consequence of a big snarl-up of tanks and trucks behind the lines, which hindered the closure of the Falaise Pocket, General Eisenhower demoted him.

[78]   Major General Fay B. Prickett, USMA '14, and Brigadier General Albert C. Stanford, USMA '17, of the Seventy-fifth Infantry Division, were relieved on January 23, 1945. As early as January 19, 1945, General Ridgway had expressed his concern about their leadership in a two-page letter to General Hodges, as the inexperienced division was not living up to General Ridgway's expectations in its initial combat in the most trying of times. The Seventy-fifth Infantry Division was the epitome of an inexperienced unit led by commanders with active service in World War I and successful careers prior to its deployment. The Seventy-fifth had arrived in France on December 13, 1944, and had been picked apart by General Collins of the US VII Corps to provide two infantry regiments to the Third Armored Division to support General Ridgway's defense of Manhay. The subsequent achievements of the Seventy-fifth and the successful careers of Generals Prickett and Stanford cast doubt on the judgment of those quick to find fault with their performance.

CHAPTER 13

[79]   The Legion of Merit is a military award given for exceptionally meritorious service. It is only one of two decorations to be issued as a "neck order," a decoration that may be worn on a ribbon around the neck. First awarded in 1942, Bailey, Banks, and Biddle created the Legion of Merit design to be similar to the French Legion of Honor.

[80]   The Hays Code is the official Hollywood code of self-censorship in place from 1930-1968, named for Will H. Hays, president of the Motion Picture Producers and Distributors of America from 1922-1945.

[81]   This is a Scottish colloquialism meaning "wee small hours" of the morning.

[82]   This quote gives an honest and humorous glimpse at the diversity of the soldiers of the US Army. All races, religions, and classes were present. By and large, with honest fits and starts, as a merit-based system, where advancement is determined by performance, the military led the way in desegregation.

[83]   Staff corps responsibilities are designated: G1 personnel; G2 military intelligence; G3 operations; G4 logistics; and G5 civil and military operations.

[84]   The Advanced Service Rating Score was a system the Army devised to determine which soldiers would be demobilized first. Months overseas, months in combat, campaign or battle stars, and awards for gallantry counted for points. High-pointers were the "lucky" few who had been overseas for long periods of time. The XVI Corps was not designated for long-term occupation duty in Germany and was scheduled to be deactivated—hence the term "Category IV."

CHAPTER 14

[85]   Simpson papers, Special Order No. 153 under covering letter Major General John A. Klein, adjutant general, advanced Lieutenant General William Simpson to full general on the retired list.

[86]   Drew Pearson, "The Washington Merry-Go-Round," *The Washington Post*, October, 5, 1961. For three decades, Drew Pearson was the most famous political writer of his day.

[87]   Ernest Harmon, USMA '17 to Mr. E.G. Davis, undated letter, Ernest N. Harmon Papers, USAMHI.

[88]   Wheeler Field was the base from which the United States Army Air Corps responded to the attack by the Japanese on December 7, 1941.

[89]   John Kennedy Ohl, *Supplying the Troops: General Somervell and American Logistics in World War II* (DeKalb, Illinois: Northern Illinois Press, 1994), 184-5.

[90]   John Toland, *The Last 100 Days* (New York: Random House, 1966).

[91]   S. L. A. Marshall was an official Army combat historian during WWII.

[92]   Cornelius Ryan, *The Last Battle* (New York: Simon & Schuster, 1966). Reference here is to the entire book.

CHAPTER 15

[93]   Mark Helprin, *A Soldier of the Great War* (Orlando, Florida: Harcourt Brace Jovanovich, 1991).

BIBLIOGRAPHY

Allen, Peter. *One More River*. New York: Charles Scribner's, 1980.

Atkinson, Rick. *The Guns at Last Light*. New York: Henry Holt and Company, 2013.

Barr, Niall. *Eisenhower's Armies*. New York: Pegasus Books, 2015.

Bennett, Donald. *Honor Untarnished*. New York: Tom Doherty Associates, 2003.

Bennett, Robert. *U.S. Army World War II Corps Commanders*. Fort Leavenworth, Kansas: Combat Studies Institute, 1989.

Bradley, Omar N. *A Soldier's Story*. New York: Henry Holt and Company, 1951.

Bradley, Omar N. and Clay Blair. *A General's Life*. New York: Simon & Schuster, 1983.

Bryant, Arthur. *Triumph in the West*. Garden City, New York: Doubleday, 1959.

Calhoun, Mark. *General Lesley J. McNair*. Lawrence, Kansas: University Press of Kansas, 2015.

Chandler, Alfred D. *The Papers of Dwight David Eisenhower. The War Years: IV*. Baltimore and London: The Johns Hopkins Press, 1970.

Chynoweth, Bradford G. *Bellamy Park: Memoirs by Bradford Grethen Chynoweth.* Hicksville, New York: Exposition Press, 1975.

Clark, Lloyd. *Crossing the Rhine.* New York: Atlantic Monthly Press, 2008.

Cohen, Roger. *Soldiers and Slaves.* New York: Alfred A. Knopf, 2005.

Danchev, Alex and Daniel Todman, eds. *War Diaries, 1939-1945. Field Marshal Lord Alanbrooke.* Berkeley and Los Angeles, California: University of California Press, 2001.

English, John A. *Patton's Peers: The Forgotten Allied Field Army Commanders of the Western Front 1944-45.* Mechanicsburg, Pennsylvania: Stackpole Books, 2009.

Ford, Ken and Howard Gerrard. *The Rhine Crossings 1945.* New York: Osprey, 2007.

Fuermann, George M. and F. Edward Cranz. *Ninety-Fifth Infantry Division History 1918-1946.* Atlanta: Albert Love Enterprises, 1945.

Fussell, Paul. *The Boys' Crusade. American G.I.s in Europe: Chaos and Fear in World War Two.* London: Weidenfeld & Nicolson, 2004.

Hastings, Max. *Armageddon: The Battle for Germany, 1944-1945.* New York: Alfred A. Knopf, 2004.

Irving, David. *The War Between the Generals: Inside the Allied High Command.* New York: Congdon & Lattes, 1981.

Jeffers, H. Paul. *Taking Command: General J. Lawton Collins from Guadalcanal to Utah Beach to Victory in Europe.* New York: New American Library, 2009.

Hewitt, Robert L. *Work Horse of the Western Front: The Story of the 30th Infantry Division.* Washington: Infantry Journal Press, 1946.

Hobbs, Joseph P. *Dear General: Eisenhower's Wartime Letters to Marshall.* Baltimore and London: The Johns Hopkins University Press, 1971.

Lavin, Frank. *Home Front to Battlefront: An Ohio Teenager in World War II.* Athens: Ohio University Press, 2016.

MacDonald, Charles B. *The Last Offensive: U.S. Army in World War II European Theater of Operations.* Atlanta: Whitman Publishing, 1972.

Mick, Allan H. *With the 102nd Infantry Division Through Germany.* Washington: Infantry Journal Press, 1947.

Miller, Edward G. *Nothing Less Than Full Victory. Americans at War in Europe, 1944-1945.* Annapolis: Naval Institute Press, 2007.

Morelock, Jerry D. *Generals of the Bulge. Leadership in the U.S. Army's Greatest Battle.* Mechanicsburg, Pennsylvania: Stackpole Books, 2015.

Morgan, Kay Summersby. *Past Forgetting. My Love Affair with Dwight D. Eisenhower.* New York: Simon and Schuster, 1975.

Nichol, John and Tony Rennell. *The Last Escape. The Untold Story of Allied Prisoners of War in Europe 1944-45.* New York: Viking, 2002.

Parker, Theodore W. and William J. Thompson. *Conquer: The Story of Ninth Army.* Washington: Infantry Journal Press, 1947.

Plokhy, Serhii M. *Yalta. The Price of Peace.* New York: Viking, 2010.

Stock, James W. *Rhine Crossing.* New York: Ballantine, 1973.

Sylvan, William C. and Francis G. Smith. *Normandy to Victory. The War Diary of General Courtney H. Hodges & the First U.S. Army.* Lexington: The University Press of Kentucky, 2008.

Taafe, Stephen R. *Marshall and His Generals: U.S. Army Commanders in World War II.* Lawrence, Kansas: University Press of Kansas, 2011.

Weigley, Russell F. *Eisenhower's Lieutenants: The Campaigns of France and Germany, 1944-1945.* Bloomington: Indiana University Press, 1981.

Wheeler, James S. *Jacob L. Devers: A General's Life.* Lexington: The University Press of Kentucky, 2015.

Whiting, Charles. *Battle of the Ruhr Pocket.* New York: Ballantine Books, 1970.

Winton, Harold R. *Corps Commanders of the Bulge: Six American Generals and Victory in the Ardennes.* Lawrence, Kansas: University Press of Kansas, 2007.

Wyche, Ira T. *The Cross of Lorraine. A Combat History of the 79th Infantry Division, June 1942-December 1945.* Knoxville: The Battery Press, 1945.

ACKNOWLEDGMENTS

M any thanks are due to many people for this book. I was first seriously inspired to write it upon reading Frank Lavin's book about his father's World War II service, *Home Front to Battlefront*. My daughter Emma K. Van Ness, PhD, has my love and admiration for her encouragement to go beyond a dry recitation of diary entries and letters and to focus instead on my grandfather's state of mind during the momentous events he witnessed. My friends Peter Craig of Landon School days and Brooke Anderson of the Ohio Military Museum and the Military Aircraft Preservation Society of Canton, Ohio, read the early manuscript critically and pushed me to improve it. Along with the rejection letters of university press editors, these criticisms made the book better.

Without the ongoing, faithful encouragement of my wife, Sandra E. Soni, the book would never have been completed. Her unwavering support included reformatting text, inserting and deleting photos and endnotes, and delving into the arcane world of Microsoft Word. At times an "author's widow," she never once failed to send me back to the keyboard to complete another necessary task. For these reasons and more, I am so very grateful.

CPSIA information can be obtained
at www.ICGtesting.com
Printed in the USA
LVHW111951170220
647203LV00003B/305

9 781633 938496